Moorland and Stream
by William Barry

Address:
HardPress
8345 NW 66TH ST #2561
MIAMI FL 33166-2626
USA
Email: info@hardpress.net

MOORLAND AND STREAM.

MOORLAND AND STREAM.

WITH

NOTES AND PROSE IDYLS

ON

SHOOTING AND TROUT FISHING,

By W. BARRY.

LONDON:
INSLEY BROTHERS, 18, CATHERINE ST., STRAND.
1871.

PRINTED BY TAYLOR AND CO.,
LITTLE QUEEN STREET, LINCOLN'S INN FIELDS.

NOTICE.

THE chapters in this Volume entitled " Pictures from an Irish Moorland " have been reprinted, by permission, from the ' PALL MALL GAZETTE.'

SLOANE STREET,
 June 24th, 1871.

CONTENTS.

PICTURES FROM AN IRISH MOORLAND.

PICTURES FROM THE "WISP."

NOTES ON SHOOTING.

TROUT FISHING.

AN IDYL OF THE "WIMPLE."

A MAY IDYL.

MY FISHING COMPANIONS.

NOTES ON TROUT FISHING.

PICTURES FROM AN IRISH MOORLAND.

CHAPTER I.

SHAUN RUADHA.

In the dark hour before dawn of a December morning the moorland fowler slips shivering into the gloomy car that in Ireland is called covered.   His way is through the street of an old ramshackle town, in which a dank sea fog muffles the gas lamps, while his vehicle is at every moment interrupted by the warning shout of a peasant driving a sort of tumbril full of pigs intended for sale at the monthly market held on the edge of the borough.   Though the day has not yet broken, the pig fair is in full swing; lights twinkle from the tents, the intractable grunters are growling and squeaking on all sides, the road is blocked in Lud-

B

gate Hill fashion by a congestion of traffic
unmistakably of a Celtic and agricultural cha-
racter. And now the sportsman escapes towards
the ascent to the moors, or mountains, as they
are termed in the district. From the summit
he can see a faint green tinge chilling out the
stars in the east, and he knows that the grey
dim expanse underneath is the side to which
even thus early·certain wading birds are wend-
ing their flight and exchanging pass-words and
challenges with each other overhead. Gradually,
as if they had been muffled in brown holland
and then stripped by degrees, the hedgerows,
the dark plumes of the fir, the couched cattle
and sheep, the dirty, picturesque cabins, come
into view. Day arrives at last, sulky and re-
luctant. The moor-fowl shooter has reached
his starting-point where the cunning Shaun
Ruadha (Red John) awaits him with the dogs.
The " covered car " is consigned with its coach-
man to the hospitality of a farmer resident on
the skirts of a wet desert, on which four lean kine
are wistfully meditating on the miseries of star-
vation. The farmer himself wishes the shooter
" good luck," while Shaun, eager as the setters

for the sport, twirls in his hand the "taste of a stick" with which he is wont to beat for a hare or a woodcock in the way of business, or to employ for recreation in a humorous skull-breaking game, which not unfrequently comes off at the cross-road village beyond. Shaun thinks it better to charge with heavy shot, and steal as quietly as possible towards a sure find that he knows for wild ducks. A snipe, bleating loudly, starts from the rushes, but the nobler quarry in prospect has saved him from a chance of being the first tenant of the day's bag. A loutish heron, with a bronchitic snuffle, flops out of a ditch. The fowler and his henchman dread that the whutter made by the long-legged angler will frighten the mallards and their nervous companions; but no, if they are here they have not taken any notice of either heron or snipe. The fowler has directed that Bob and Nell, the setters, should be tied and kept in hand by Shaun, as the patter of their feet might discover the movement projected. Alas! this piece of strategy is fatal to the success of the undertaking. Bob is shaking and trembling with sheer excitement, and for his

very life cannot suppress a whimpering petition
for release to join actively in the fun.   At the
instant there is a rush of pinions, and seven
wild duck have put themselves well out of shot
before their whereabouts has been distinctly
ascertained.   And so there is no longer any
use in keeping in the dogs, and they com-
mence to range the soaked and sodden marsh.
Bob has only coursed round a single turn when
he throws his head aloft, and then marches
gravely to a solitary tuft of tall bog-grass, and
becomes as fixed as marble before it.   Nell
from afar off imitates his deportment, and then
Shaun advances to perform his part, and as he
thwacks the grass puss dashes from her retreat,
and at thirty yards is stopped with the best
part of an ounce and a quarter of No. 8.

Why does Shaun of a sudden (he not being
at all in the line of fire) tumble flat on his face
and begin to whistle?   Behold! in the air a
great army of golden plover already hearkening
and replying to the shrill, querulous piping of
the cunning Shaun.   The squadron has its
scouts, its Uhlans, its wary videttes, but is with-
drawn so far from earth at present that it defies

attack, and is engaged perhaps in a grand re-
connaissance of the barren stony parish over
which it wheels and cries. Shaun, *ventre à
terre*, continues to whistle, and at length his
perseverance is rewarded by a detachment of
the birds floating down in narrowing circuits
responding to his call. Nearer and nearer the
doomed contingent approaches to where Shaun
and his watchful master are in readiness to re-
ceive them; their comrades in the clouds sus-
pect that matters are not right, and begin to
clamour in a warning key to the rash division
that has parted from them. Bang! bang!
four down; and a fifth winged who has just
fallen into yonder pool.

Here the moorland is comparatively dry. It
is covered with withered ferns and broom, and
at the pressure of the foot yields a perfume of
new-mown hay and cinnamon. At times you
meet a bunch of some sort of berry, the name
of which would be more useful to poets than
the cherries they compare the lips of fair
women to, and the burning red contrasts finely
with the tints of the heather and the scattered
blocks of moss-crusted granite. Shaun ob-

serves none of these things, but practically re-
marks that, " Av there's a cock in the wurrld,
there's won to be got " in the neighbourhood,
and he proceeds to trample and flog briar and
bramble and roar, " Hie, cock! hie, cock;"
with vehemence, until he abandons the exer-
cise through sheer exhaustion. The dogs are
not able to do much on account of the tangle
of thorns; but just as Shaun temporarily rests
from his labours both are setting on the barest
track in the place. " 'Tis a cock for sartain,"
whispers Shaun, " and mebbe two. Steady,
Bob!" Bob is as steady as a rock, Nell backs
with a rigidity of manner that is admired after
its fashion in a duchess as well as in a setter,
the moor fowler with hand on trigger is pre-
pared for the flushing of a glorious addition to
supper, and a wretched Jack-snipe jerks from
under Bob's nose, and goes away unmolested.
Later on, however, fortune is kinder to the
sportsman, and a couple of cock reward him
for his perseverance, together with two brace
of snipe. These birds with changes of weather
shift their haunts from the low marshy grounds
to the drier uplands, but frequent the moist

grounds during the night. Shaun could tell you accurately enough the habits of snipe; and though unable to bring them down with a gun, will never fail to procure a number of them to order. The rascal snares them with ingeniously planted rods, on which the snipe are made literally to hang themselves; and you may occasionally find a dozen of the engines pitched close to an oozing spring situated within the range of Mr. Shaun's usual wanderings. The fellow will only spend powder and shot on wild duck or on the golden plover; among the latter he makes tremendous havoc in strong gales, or at eventide, when he creeps to the lonely side of the mountain on which the birds assemble for the night.

The moorland shooter in December must not expect the comfortable proportions of game which are almost assured to the fowler who takes a grouse-stocked moor in August. The prospect of a good bag is always near and probable enough to give an interest to the expedition for making it, while the chances of complete failure impart a zest to every little success achieved. When the dusk has warned the fowler off the hills, he counts over with Shaun a couple of woodcock, a heavy duck, a teal, three brace of plover, four of snipe, a hare, and a green plover (pewit); and then departs into the gathering gloom, with an appetite for dinner that is in itself worth coming from Pall Mall to Rhein Dhuv to experience. How long the road seems, how slow the horse ! And what ruffians are those who interrupt our route, who, having sold their pigs, are now as drunken as the sow of David in the bottom of their abominable waggons ! But the lights of the town are visible at length, and as the car again rattles through the streets the sportsman glances back on the hills, now silvered with the shine of the moon, and is exceedingly rejoiced to leave them, poetry, Shaun, game, and all, in order to eat tender mutton, and put his weary legs under a bright sparkling table.

CHAPTER II.

ANDY COTTER.

In order to traverse the wilderness of Monarrogue, the assistance of Andy Cotter is absolutely requisite. A fair portion of this profitable estate is under water for three months in the year; the rest is composed of heather and stones, with small intervals of cultivated fields in which turnips are occasionally visible to the naked eye. Mr. Cotter is tenant for as much almost of this earthly paradise as you can see. Where the hill of Knocknagow sleeps in the shape of a couched mastiff against the skyline, Andy has erected a sort of cairn of granite to mark the boundary of his farm, and on the slope of Knocknagow itself the family mansion of the Cotters shrinks within an enclosure of stunted firs. From the vale below rises a dank perpetual mist, through which you may catch a glimpse of one or two of the five lean kine possessed by Andy roaming emptily about in search of the rations which serve to keep them at starvation point. You need not fear that the cows will frighten either the wild duck, the snipe, or the hares. The wild fowl are familiar with the wretched cattle who pant and stagger through the gloomy marsh, or stand with hungry wistful looks on the edge of a pool, sending now and again into the air a melancholy moan, in reply, as it were, to the scream of the frantic pewits who are tumbling overhead in sheer delight and high spirits at the prospect of quarters so suited to their desolate habits. As you approach the dwelling of Andy Cotter the good man beholds you from afar, and sticking the spade in the garden-ooze which conceals a rare potato, advances to greet the fowler, and invite him to the hospitalities of his mansion. The interior of the Villa Cotter is so clouded with turf-smoke, that on entering it your eyes are filled with tears, and you are only conscious of a fine glow in a corner, of the voice of Mrs. Cotter giving you welcome, and of a smothered grunt of mingled jealousy and surprise from a pig in that stage of favour which immediately precedes his being sold at the fair. By-and-by you begin to distinguish objects in the Villa Cotter. The mistress of the house is a comely, good-natured looking creature, prematurely old from sharing in the labours of her husband. She may not be, probably is not, twenty, but the climate of Monarrogue and of Knocknagow tells upon the complexion. There are no children in the grimy den, but a troop of turkeys are gobble-wobbling in a corner, having been brought in for a mess-parade, and a jackass, who has been contemplating a green duck-pond before the hall door, darkens the entrance with an intention of joining the company, which is frustrated by a word in Irish to him from his master. The poor couple produce a bowl of milk, and offer it pressingly to the stranger, and Mrs. Cotter smilingly places next to it a soda-water bottle full of whisky and a loaf of brown bread. Whereupon (the stranger not venturing on the vulgarity of entirely refusing the delicacies put before him) the conversation inclines to the business of wild-fowl shooting. In a few minutes Andy has furnished himself with a blackthorn stick for " beating " the ground, and with " A good day's sport to you, Sir," from Mrs. Cotter, the shooter commences his operations by transferring the game bag to the broad shoulders of his guide.

We are soon on the higher steeps of Knock-nagow, knee-deep in broom. Close to the boundary cairn is a circular lakelet, not unlike the crater of an extinct volcano. Towards the edge of this we creep with the utmost caution, stopping for a moment to seek some oral evidence that our quarry is on the water. A slight exclamation of pain as a thorn runs into the leg of the fowler startles a vigilant teal from its surface, and the pretty little bird springs up with an alarmed flutter and wheels cautiously out of distance, but decides that all is safe, and returns to its resting-place. Nevertheless, suspecting that bigger game may be had, the fowler stops in his ascent in order to allay suspicion of his approach. Hark to the intermittent wild clamour of a pack of foxhounds far down the other side of Knocknagow :—

> " Matched in mouth-like bells
> Each under each."

The noise of the chase has a queer dim sound, now a frolicsome outburst and full chorus, now the challenge of a single dog, a long reach of joyous cadences, two bars rest, and the whole lot are at it again, while the wind gives a fitful emphasis or softness to the concert that accords so effectively with the savage landscape. The fowler and his guide, having reached the edge of the pond, are gratified with the sight of four wild duck and a brace of their tiny kindred, the teal, playfully, and with no apparent dread of human interruption, disporting themselves on its gleaming inky round. As the smoke from the barrels clears away, two of the heavy birds are seen to have fallen. The fading hues on the neck of the mallard (they seem to fade at any rate) outrival the glories of a pigeon's neck, or the bravest gem in the tail of Juno's chariot peacock. The duck, with-brown and mottled dress, is far more simply clothed. Yet her brilliant companion is the most constant and affectionate of husbands, and is content with the companionship of his homely wife long after that period which corresponds with the time of the white glove on the knocker among the featherless bipeds. Pipes are solemnly smoked after the mallard and duck have been consigned to the bag, and

a consultation as to the next route is called.
"'Tis no good tryin' Rhein after the wet last
night," Mr. Cotter opines; "Knocknagerah is
perhaps too far, but Murphy's Bog is just the
place for us."

Monarrogue is, God knows, as Andy Cotter
fervently remarked, "a dissholute (desolate)
bit o' land;" but how is Murphy's Bog to be
described? The very mountains that encom-
pass Murphy's Bog are perpetually in tears. A
brook sighs through the centre of it, gurgling
the most melancholy water-music. Murphy's
Bog groans of its own motion at times, and
the placing of your foot on the morass is a
signal for a lugubrious gamut of soughs and
murmurs which warn you not to take liberties
with a district that is reported to have swal-
lowed in a single gulp two infantry officers who
without guides came after snipe to the spot.
Their ghosts are said to haunt the place at
night, their guns explode without noise, and
leave a stronger smell of sulphur after the per-
formance than is noticeable in the ammunition
made by Pigou, or Curtis and Harvey. As
the unfortunate gentlemen were Protestants,

the supernatural whiff of sulphur in their powder is supposed to be a matter of course. Andy Cotter can bring you through Murphy' Bog without the water at any time coming much higher than your breeches pockets. Andy invites you to jump with him from tuft to tuft, and flies like an acrobat from one mound of quaking, grumbling moss to another, which wobbles with your weight, and appears to roar under you. Shooting under the circumstances is not so easy. To be sure, the snipe are plenty; but it puzzles a good dog to get them when hit, and they are oftener missed than otherwise as you are canting and balancing yourself over a possible peat-grave in Murphy's Bog. Andy is content to show you the birds; hitting or missing is your own affair; but he is certain at the close of the day to remind you of all you saw, and how little comparatively you are possessed of. The rascal is villanously honest and remorselessly candid. "That's the second hare wud a white scut we missed to-day, Sir," he calls out after the repetition of—well, an accident, in Murphy's Bog. And he gazes with an aggravating expression of sorrow at the twinkling flanks of puss, who is off to Knocknagerah, with a speed that seems to have an air of practical irony in it. Subsequently the fowler, emerging from the perilous reaches of Murphy's Bog, manages to win even compliments from Andy Cotter. Andy is gifted with an extra faculty for the discovery of forms and hare tracks. The dervish of the Eastern tale, who told that the horse was lame and carried a load of honey from merely examining the footmarks of the animal, was a fool to Andy Cotter as he stoops over a hare track, and tells you when the hare was there last, whether she was going or coming, and where she is likely to be put up. Snipe Andy regards as not worth pursuit; but he is learned as to the haunts of these fowl, and is quite equal to a dog in finding dead. As we turn our faces from Murphy's Bog the dusk has begun to fall around, and a wan fragment of moon creeps up on the ridge of Monarrogue. The evening is frosty, and every other minute as the night comes on, the sky sparkles with stars, and Andy astonishes the fowler with a display of small astronomical lore, such as a recognition of the better known constellations. There was not much of the Chaldean shepherd in Andy, but he had acquired his taste for star learning through a hedge schoolmaster, whose academy was calculated for studies in the open, and who held a night class for those who had not the leisure to take instructions from him during the day. As we trudged homewards, Andy suddenly halted to call attention to the whistle of duck, and proposes a return for half an hour or so to Murphy's Bog on chance of a shot. This proposition is by no means cheerfully received. Mrs. Cotter has placed a candle in the window of Monarrogue cabin, and as the kindly taper shines a welcome from the black bulk of the hill, the notion of a retrograde march to Murphy's Bog—mayhap to catch the ague, or behold the ghostly warriors stalking their appointed vigil—does not recommend itself to the exhausted and hungry sportsman. At Monarrogue the fowler has his car in waiting and ready to convey him from the bleak wilderness, after a farewell from Andy and his partner, and a wish expressed from the former

that it won't be long before Monarrogue and
Murphy's Bog are laid under contribution for
game again.

CHAPTER III.

THE BARONY OF THREENEHEILA WITHIN DRUM.*

THREENEHEILA in the red morning, when the
snow on the shadowy Galtees is tinged with a
crimson flush, and when the green waters of
the tide lap the hedge of the fir covert in
which the herons are yet snoozing, has not
that air of unfriendly desolation which marks
the Irish moorland generally. Cabins are plen-
tifully dotted over it. You have within view
a disestablished church, a police barrack, a
chapel, a national school-house, and a marine
village with a coastguard flag floating in the
vicinity of one of those archæological conun-
drums, a round tower, about whose origin the
antiquarians have been quaintly speculative.
Threeneheila is celebrated for a saint who lived

* Within "Drum" or "droun," *i.e.* within certain
heads (headlands), which formed boundary marks.

in the parish in or near the days of Patrick, and whose name has been conferred so frequently on the peasants that the circumstance, coupled with the fact that the inhabitants are nearly all Sullivans or Flynns, gives rise to an enormous amount of confusion touching the use of the franchise at election times. The place is also rich in holy wells, in legends thereanent, and perhaps the last fairy doctor, who combines the functions of an herbalist and a bone-setter with his wizard accomplishments, is to be found in Threeneheila. There, too, resides a typical specimen of that fast decaying race the Squireen. The mansion of the Squireen was in former times a centre of rough-and-ready hospitality. The father of the present proprietor was a sportsman of a high order, who could not only bring down his brace of birds right and left with certainty, but who was so ready with a saw-handle Rigby on the cool grass before breakfast that he achieved the feat of driving a half-crown with a bullet from the waistcoat pocket into the stomach of his dearest friend with whom he had an unhappy difference. From his parlour window he could point to the field in which he has broken the leg of an English gentleman with whom he had a dispute at a hunt dinner; and it was thought extremely good-natured of Mr. Dwyer to have aimed low on the occasion. He was always in debt, but no bailiff could be got to serve him with a legal process. It was reported he had dogs with a nose for a catch-pole who would give tongue as soon as ever the bearer of a king's writ put his leg in the parish. He had a grand wake and funeral at his death, was universally regretted by the country people, and left a thumping legacy of unliquidated debts, mortgages, and Chancery suits to his son, who is sincerely and affectionately vain of the talents and virtues of his good father.

The Lodge of Threeneheila has seen better days. There are signs and tokens of a flower garden having been before the hall door, there are ragged ramshackle remnants of out-offices and stabling accommodation long disused and idle, barns abandoned even by the rats, odd gnarled apple-trees indicating the site of an orchard, artificial mounds on an acre now surrendered to the geese and the pigs suggesting a lawn, and a half-choked pool which had been an artificial pond. The roof is patched with divers-coloured slates, and ghastly daubs of whitewash streak the venerable chocolate hue of the walls. The chimneys lean on one side, the inevitable pigs roam freely around the premises, and on the top of a broken dismantled cart an indefatigable cock appears to be ceaselessly crowing in his loudest voice defiant challenges to another bashaw who keeps guard on a contiguous midden. Issuing from this interesting Lodge the wild-fowl shooter is accompanied by his host, who also carries a gun, and has at his heels a pointer as like the spectre of a dog as the hideous quadruped depicted by Hogarth in one of the pictures of " Marriage à la Mode." Billy the pointer has a pedigree almost as respectable as that of his master, but before an hour is over he proves that his education has been sadly neglected, though his his relish for the pastime in which he assisted was instinctively keen. Billy the pointer is set out to work in a wood covered with an undergrowth of brown ferns which yield the most delicious perfume to the pressure of the feet. The brute works with energy and skill. *Mark!* Up springs a woodcock and is stopped by Dwyer as he darts for his life between a silver larch and a rowan; quick as lightning Billy pounces on the fallen bird, and rends him as the beagles would a fox. Tom Dwyer curses as the army never did in Flanders; he bellows for Billy to come and be flogged; but Billy regards us both from a safe distance, blood and feathers smeared on his maw, and an expression of stolid innocence or indifference on his countenance. The woodcock is reduced to mere pulp and a pair of legs, and the mess presented by what was a wild-fowl again provokes a renewal of strong language from Mr. Dwyer, the glib command of which a Thames bargeman might envy. We get three couple of cock from the wood after driving Billy away, and then Dwyer proposes that we should watch in the "bawn" fields for the golden plover.

The "bawn" fields are no sooner reached than we hear the low pipe of the birds, which are to be distinguished from big thrushes and starling at any distance from the fact of their invariably running instead of hopping. Peeping carefully over the hedge we arrange to creep to opposite sides of the enclosure and then start the birds, which are thickly massed in the middle of it. Just as we are on the point of executing the movement Billy the pointer appears on the scene and jumps and races at the stand with a malicious and desperate eagerness. With a howl of rage Tom Dwyer makes towards him, and it is well for Billy that he has sense enough to keep out of range of Tom's old Manton. But later on we are thoroughly successful with the plover. Again and again the birds return to the fields, at the corners of which we are able to intercept them. We leave a wounded plover on the ground as a decoy, and his wailing companions wheel down from the very clouds—snow clouds—in circles about him. When the sun has burned down in the west our bags are loaded in every pocket, and shooting a wild duck in the glen near the wood we have to carry him by hand, so completely have our creels been filled.

On Threeneheila is a lone dismal lough, on which forms the smoothest ice a skater could desire. In the moonlight, after a homely but by no means despicable dinner at the Lodge, Tom Dwyer and his guest start for the lough, and after carefully inspecting one end of it for traces of a string of wild geese which have been reported in the neighbourhood, are quickly shod with the necessary steels. The moon makes queer shadows as its rim rests on the shoulder of the Galtees; the cold is intense, and after a turn or so, the gurgle from Tom's flask is not unpleasant music. As he sheers off by himself his tall figure appears to flicker in the green haze, and save for the noise of the skates the silence is intense, while every star is visible in the arch overhead, their aching distances shown by the vast reaches of shining dust that seem to be still so much further from us. After an hour on the lough we prepare to return to the Lodge by another route from that by which we came. There is a smithy by the roadside, into which we go to light a pipe. The trestle around the bellows of Leum Gow is crowded; this is the gossip club of the parish. There are eight or ten men in the place besides the brawny Leum (William) himself, and one woman. The woman is a brazen, hard-looking wench, a female pedlar, who hawks needles, thread, cheap looking-glasses, pious pictures, almanacs, hair-pins, ballads, of the most humble pattern, through the country. The lady is known as " Biddy the Rambler," and is not popular, despite the convenience of her calling, with the honest wives of the neighbourhood. Biddy has a pair of bold black eyes, and smokes a dhudeen with evident and quite unaffected pleasure in the weed. Tom Dwyer and his guest are tempted to· linger for a quarter of an hour in this strange company, whose shyness at their advent wore off after a hearty exchange of Irish phrases of welcome with the former. Biddy presses some of her wares on the stranger, who offers to buy a dozen of the ballads if any one present will sing a sample from the collection for him. Leum Gow was appealed to by Biddy as a boy that could " rise it," and Leum was nothing loth. The smoke and ashes of his trade had not in the least impaired a voice that was of a quality rather capable of improvement than the reverse, by being, as it were, a little muffled in soot.   Leum, being able to read, got a sheaf of ballads to select from, but after looking at the titles he gave two to the purchaser of the broad-sheets, and then commenced to render them one after another, exhibiting a perfect acquaintance with the text. Here are a few excerpts from the singular compositions intoned by this harmonious blacksmith.   The first was termed :—

THE PRAISES OF ROCKBARTON.

Could I indite like Horace, Virgil, Homer, Ovid,
Or had I the talents of Plato or Socrates,
I'd strive to praise Rockbarton where resides the Lord
    Chief Baron.
There you'll see the linnet coequal with the spinnet,
The blackbird every minute chanting forth his lay,
The turtle and the pigeon, the cuckoo sweetly singing,
 The woodcock and the widgeon sequestered in the
    shade,
All singing like an organ in praise of Rockbarton,
And wishing his Lordship's offspring may there for
    ever reign !

The second was named "Sweet Colleen Rhue." The opening stanza runs thus :—

As I roved out on a summer morning
A-speculating most curiously,
To my surprise I soon espied
A charming fair one approaching.
I stood awhile in meditation
Contemplating what I should do,
Till at length, recruiting all my sinsations,
I then accosted the Colleen Rhue.

When Leum Gow concluded his song he was heartily applauded, but could not be induced to attempt a third ballad. We leave the smithy with a regular chorus of friendly wishes sent after us. There is a stewed hare for supper at Threeneheila, and over the subsequent rest before the peat-fire another day's campaign is projected. Tom Dwyer is with difficulty prevented from passing sentence of death on Billy the pointer. He is dreadfully ashamed of Billy's behaviour, and protests he never knew the dog to break fence, to run at shot, or to spring the birds before. He was bred from a stock kept up on Threeneheila for fifty years, and is the last of his tribe. His offences, however, have deserved capital punishment. "Here, Billy!" roars the master of the Lodge, and Billy enters the room, and, instead of chastisement, receives a hare bone, which he crunches under the table. One may guess the same scene is repeated pretty often, for Dwyer is attached to the blundering old dog. No need of lotos, stuffed pillows, or sleeping syrup of Nepenthes, after such a day as this; to touch the bed is at once to sink into complete rest, undisturbed except by a morning dream of Biddy the Rambler singing with Leum Gow the "Praises of Rockbarton" at a Crystal Palace concert.

CHAPTER IV.

"IN THE HARD GREY WEATHER."

THE iron grip of the frost is on the fen, and the bitter north-east wind whistles through the reeds and rushes, drowning even the roar of the sea which beats sullenly on the edge of the moor:—

> The Cormorant on high
> Wheels from the deep and screams along the land;
> Loud shrieks the soaring hern, and with wild wing
> The circling sea-fowl cleave the flaky clouds.

The great grey gulls have flown so far land-
ward, and are endeavouring to tack against
the breeze and make for the red ploughed
fields on the hills. The sun is hidden behind
clouds of mingled black and yellow, with rifts
between them of steel blue; the cold is so
intense and piercing that the fowler finds it
difficult to keep his fingers fit for feeling the
triggers of the gun. The weather has been
too much for the wild-fowl themselves. At an
immense height you hear the troubled clang-
ing of a string of geese driven from the bleak
howling shore; the snipe are startled from
their sedentary habits, and are twirling and
bleating in irregular batches, seeking for a
glimpse of a spring or a stream; widgeon,
plover, and curlew are all on the move, but
keep cautiously out of range. The fowler
trudges for miles, a shivering and whimpering
setter at his heels, without getting a shot.
The dangerous traps and crosses of the bog
are now perfectly safe for passage, but every
footstep sounds on them like a thump on a
drumhead. And to make the way more weariful
by degrees the flouting companionship of the

breeze dies off, the birds cease to call, the atmosphere grows chiller and darker, and heavy flakes of snow tumble down. Arriving at a turf stack the fowler crouches at the lee side of it for shelter, and finds that he has to share the situation with a miserable ague-stricken dealer in matting and brushes, who comes on the wold to gather the material for his commerce. The poor wretch's hands are literally bleeding from contact with the frozen grass and withies; his cadaverous grimy face is livid; the December blast smites him through the thin scarecrow garments in which he cowers. The sight of this cheerless forlorn creature, who had not even the spirit to ask for alms, is too much to be borne in addition to the snow, and the fowler therefore adventures to search out a road that passes through the fen at some little distance on. As he gains this point on his route he meets with a second exhilarating prospect. A funeral conducted at a brisk trot passes along the road, the bright deal coffin having a peculiarly garish and startling emphasis stretched on the gloom of the sepulchral van on which it goes jolting. A woman in a hooded cloak is seated

at the foot of the coffin, and seems to be the
only mourner at the ceremony. What a day
to be buried among the docks and darnels of
Scullahone graveyard, a cemetery within earshot
of the melancholy ocean, on whose tombstones
the cormorants come unmolested to digest
their dinners! Here is the road-side cabin of
the widow Brien. The widow Brien is famous
for rearing turkeys, and there is a legend ex-
tant that she once raised a turkey of such size
and power that an enterprising bocogh (cripple)
purchased him for yoking to a sledge, in which
the monster fowl used to draw him at fairs and
other festive gatherings. The widow Brien
dusts a chair for the weatherbound sportsman,
and—not being unused to such offices—pre-
sents him with a towel to dry his gun with.
A Government functionary—a gentleman who
drives her Majesty's mail through a gap in the
postal railway service of the district—is refresh-
ing himself at the hearth by making love to
the widow Brien's daughter. The girl is a
small healthy brunette, with liquid brown eyes
and little hands—the nuttiest of nut-brown
maids, with an arch, shy, coquettish welcome

for the stranger, as though she were ready enough to play him off for half an hour or so with her stout admirer, whose red "trap" has been put up in the rear of the dwelling. But the day has suddenly cleared up, the snow has ceased to fall, and the sun has managed to get a chance of shining over the forlorn landscape. The fowler takes a comprehensive and strategic survey of the ground, and decides on moving seawards, where the springs are more frequent and the salt in the marsh prevents the snipe haunts from being altogether locked and clamped by the frost.

An artificial bank runs along a creek in which the tide is now at its full. The water is turbid and continues to lap and surge against the wall of the protecting fence, as though it were training to leap the barrier it has often before triumphantly assailed. In the middle of the fiord are several diminutive islands, on which thousands and tens of thousands of sea-birds are whuttering and screaming in a perpetual clamour and Babel of shrieks. They are, of course, quite unapproachable; and, indeed, with few exceptions, would not be worth an expenditure of cartridges.   Occasionally, however, a flock of the grey sand-plover rises from the feathered mass, and these may be drawn within range by a skilful imitation of their piping.   The sand-plover is a good bird for the spit, about the same size as the golden plover, but with a grey instead of a dark coating of feathers.   Red-shank may be had in similar fashion, but the red-shank cannot be recommended for table save in August, and then only when cooked out of all personal identity.   The fowler on such a beat as is here described must not be over particular if he wants to make a respectable bag, and must be content to have fish mixed with flesh in the netting.   He may be compensated by an odd heavy duck or teal, and with a few snipe from the pungent marshes.

The end of the embankment is now reached, and the fowler is face to face with the open sea.   The coast is wild and savage.   There are many scores on the wreck chart annually entered against this shallow treacherous reach, and for miles you can see the furious breakers, rank behind rank, until the farthest seems to bristle

D

and toss on the very verge of the horizon.
Wooden breakwaters had been erected along the
sands, but in a few years the gnawing "white-
toothed waves," as they are termed in an Irish
poem, had eaten up the greater part of these de-
fences, and they now attest the inefficient charac-
ter of the engineering scheme under which they
were constructed.   It is a wonder that the pea-
santry who reside in this neighbourhood do not
become duck-footed, like Nicholas the Diver.
They spend a considerable portion of their
dull uninteresting lives apparently raking in the
weed—used to manure the unkind soil which
is with difficulty kept from relapsing into pri-
mitive barrenness.   They collect cockles on
the rocks when the tide is out, and the women
gather an unpleasant slimy stuff not unknown
in London as laver.   This mess is much re-
lished on the spot with potatoes and sprats.

As the fowler tramps through the sand he
meets scores of men and women dragging from
the reluctant sea the weeds cast up by the
previous night's storm.   They pursue their
work in silence, in a moody, listless manner,
and one of the operators employs a " rake "

with only two teeth, which is about as service-
able in answering his requirements as a single-
horned bootjack for any purpose. Some of the
women wear petticcats as short as the garments
of the Boulogne fisnwives, and their limbs are
as ruddy as the legs of French partridges
from being constantly pickled in the sea brine.
Most of them look what they are—the drudg-
ing helpmates of field labourers; a few have
retained a certain comeliness of aspect, which
will not last long under the hard struggle for
food and shelter they are obliged to go through.

The hard grey weather has grown if possible
harder during the night; and next day at
dawn the fowler is up and off to a different
moorland, accompanied by a little man who
has a sincere faith in Robinson Crusoe and
Indian adventures. The excursion has a won-
derfully romantic air to this bright urchin, who
is very learned in the details of savage practices
(as related in boys' story books), and who pro-
poses at an early hour to pluck a snipe and
cook him over a fire of reeds. He has brought
a box of matches in his pocket for the pur-
pose, conceding that we had lost the art of

making a fire by rubbing sticks together, and is scarce reconciled to a rejection of his idea even when presented with a wedge of plum cake.   He stalks bravely through the heather in buoyant spirits at the gamekeeperishness of his costume, for he has been gaitered for the occasion, and has been solemnly trusted and invested with the dog-whistle and the dog-whip.   A serious difficulty however arises with him on the subject of a winged woodcock. He pleads hard to be allowed to bring the bird home for a pet, and tries to tempt the appetite of the poor wounded fowl with a morsel of plum-cake.   He regards the quick and necessary killing of the cock with looks and expressions of reproach altogether inconsistent with his subsequent enjoyment of clean shooting at snipe and hares.

When the fowler arrives at a frozen lakelet, he finds that the ice will bear, and, having provided for such a contingency, is soon sheering and skimming over the surface of the pond.   But again, as on the previous day, the snow commences to fall, and here much thicker than on the low lands.   So the skates are unscrewed, and a cast is made for the nearest farm. The lad is charmed with the snow, and his head is full of Arctic voyages, while his tongue is wagging on the same text. He has a secret ambition—coyly revealed—to be an Esquimaux, and apparently hopes to arrive at that exalted station in life when big enough. His prattle lulls when the farm-house is reached, and he is vexed at being an object of rustic surprise and grinning wonder to Tim Callaghan. Tim pronounces that the snow will continue until dark, so the fowler and his companion are conveyed home, the driver of the car drawing the curtains closely round them, and mounting his box pelted by the flakes which fall faster and thicker every minute. Before the journey is concluded the harsh clatter and jingle of the vehicle is ex-changed for a noiseless velvety sliding over the snow-covered road, the youngster is fast asleep, and in the wonderful quiet and stillness the fowler whiles away the hour of tedious travel with a cigar.

CHAPTER V.

ON GREENLAND AT DUCK-FLIGHT.

GREENLAND consists of a brown ridge of moor —a strip from the mainland running into the sea, which is gradually eating away the desolate marsh. It seems always as bleak and as abandoned as the region of polar ice. All attempts to drain Greenland have failed utterly; it can only boast of two houses or cabins, and these are unoccupied in severe stormy weather by the miserable creatures who squat in them during the summer months. It has the reputation of a haunted district: unhallowed lights are seen there at unhallowed hours; dismal cries are heard out of the dark from Greenland on the anniversaries of shipwreck disasters which have occurred at its uttermost point. The fiery ghosts might be explained by the fact that the locality is favourable for the eccentric illuminations of Will-o'-the-Wisp; and when the equinoctial gales do blow, the perturbed shrieking and clanging of the gulls and gannets might pass for the mournful, supernatural chorus to which the peasantry refer. Cauthleen na Keenthehaun (Kate of the Keening, Kate the Keener), who lives with an idiot son within sight of Greenland, holds firmly to the weird faiths. Cauthleen is a picturesque hag who sends her poor bird-witted lad begging over the parish, where he is known as a sort of institution. Poor Cuck is a boy-man with light blue eyes, great shambling limbs, and is the happiest creature in the world. He whoops and runs over the sands, prances and chatters to the waves, gallops or trots like an unbroken colt to the neighbouring town, and is invaluable to a wild-fowl shooter as a retriever. Cuck is looked on by the people as sacred from harm or punishment; it is thought lucky to be a favourite of his; it is dangerous to vex him, for he has who knows what influence with uncanny beings who have power over the prospects of butter, of harvest, of health. Cauthleen's profession is to cry over the dead. She is one of the last of a curious race. Her keening is thought to be unusually eloquent and touching. She is regularly employed for a "wake" on the decease of a peasant whose friends can afford to pay for her accomplished services. The fowler visited Cauthleen in order to engage Cuck as a guide to Greenland for the evening. The old woman was smoking, and apparently also rehearsing a performance of her duties, for she was muttering and rocking on a stool before her hearth. Paudeen Morrissey's son had just gone off of a decline, and Paudeen wished him to be buried as those belonging to him were buried before him. The keener was conning over her task. " 'The wake was to be that night in Arvane beyant ; had his honour a drop o' whisky wid him to warm the ould woman, who knew the stock he came from ?" etc. " Och, God help us ! is it on Greenland you're goin' fowlin', an' the cold night comin' on already ! 'Tis a saying—did your honour ever hear it ?—that wheresomever the divil (God between us an' all harm) spends the day, 'tis on Greenland he spends the night ! Well, sir, Cuck can go wid ye if you're bint on it." And the withered beldame—as the old novelists would write—calls for her son, who is drawing figures with his bare big toe on the mud before the cabin door.

Cuck is delighted at being invested with the game bag, and perfectly comprehends what is required of him. Greenland is not more than half a mile away, and we shall reach it as the dusk sets in. The sun is already half sunk below the horizon, which flames over the chill glistening waters, a frigid depressing waste of grey tide unrelieved by a single sail or even the glint of a sea-bird's wing. When we arrive at the beginning of Greenland, Cuck, who is thoroughly acquainted with the grounds, leads the way to an ambush constructed of a couple of barrels sunk in the peat and filled with straw——a precaution taken that morning. Close to the kegs is a pool as black as ink, and with a sort of polished slime on its surface, and the reflection in it of a single cloud-wrack of a brazen stormy colour. Cuck nestles snugly in his barrel, peering with intense eagerness towards the western sea-line, from which we expect our quarry to come. His old battered hat is thrown off, the wind comes and blows aside his thin straw-hued hair, and his big baby eyes seem the more wistful for the momentary gleam of an unusual purpose and intention in them.   We wait a weary time, but there comes no sign or token of the birds.

As the evening grows darker and chillier, the moan of the tide rises, and a breeze starts up which increases gradually, driving a salt, penetrating mist before it which, despite the shelter of the barrel and the straw, causes one of the occupants to speculate as to whether the born fool or his employer is the greater idiot for passing such an evening on Greenland.   At length it is evident that if the wild duck did come, it would be impossible to see them; and so, crippled from long crouching, and shivering with cold, the sportsman motions to Cuck to prepare to return.   Tom o' Bedlam is as excited by the roar of the wind and sea as if he had drunk a pint of whisky.   He goes scattering odd sentences in his native tongue, of which one can only catch snatches.   His feather-brain was whirling in Edgar's fashion—" Pillicock sat on Pillicock hill.   Halloo, haloo, loo, loo !" nor would he cease his uncomfortable jabber. It was with difficulty he could be kept in sight— he would run ahead and leap a dyke, and then suddenly dash back again, clearing it with a triumphant crow at his activity, and with a challenging snap of the fingers. Not a word of the Queen's English would he speak or understand. However, he appeared to be quite certain of his route, which was a comfort under the circumstances. The Greenland ridge is at length passed, and the fowler, who has left a change of clothes at Cauthleen's cabin, is shortly knocking at the door of the mansion for admittance. A little girl with bare feet has been left in charge of the dwelling, Cauthleen having departed on her professional errand. Cuck subsides into quiet—into a sound sleep, in fact, by the side of the gaping chimney. When the stranger has warmed himself, he faces the night once more—not to go homeward, but to see the wake for which the services of Cauthleen na Keenthehaun had been retained.

Paud or Paudeen Morrissey's was a decent farmhouse. The wake took place in a large room, dimly lit, despite a blaze of candles immediately round the corpse, which was stretched on a white cloth on a table. Nothing could be more unlike the pictures and poems of Irish wakes than this reality.   There were from fifteen to twenty people present, of different ages, and most of them were on their knees praying solemnly and earnestly for the repose of the soul of the departed.   The father sat wringing his hands silently and gazing at the table with its ghastly freight; the older women, in a group, were telling their beads with hushed voices.   At times the door-latch would be raised by a new-comer, who instantly uncovered and knelt at the very threshold for a few minutes, and then took his or her place in a corner of the room without a word of greeting to those already assembled.   Paud Morrissey had designed to bring up his son as a gentleman, had him sent for schoolin' to Cork, and the lad was turning out everything his father could hope for when he caught cold from a wetting during a vacation, and lingered through the various stages of consumption until the end came at last.   The boy's mother is sobbing bitterly but not loudly; in fact, nothing can be more decorous and impressive than this house of death, until, with a sudden unexpected cry, the keener runs over to the corpse, and commences her lugubrious chant, apostrophizing the dead boy in the most startling and direct terms.   There is regular rhythm and measure in the keen, and Cauthleen is reciting the successes and achievements of young Morrissey at school.   After a while the other women are infected by the mournful appeals of Cauthleen, and they improvise on the virtues and promising acquirements of the deceased.   The visitor to this strange scene steals off quietly while the keening is at its highest pitch—the piercing minor tones following him into the blustering night almost to Cauthleen's cabin, where a vehicle is now waiting to carry him homewards.

Greenland should have been shot at moonlight, and the company of the fool was superfluous.   It was the fowler's last excursion for the season on the Irish moorlands.   The days began to grow soft, the snipe have fled to the hills, the plover keep to the mountains, the woodcock are with difficulty driven from the thickest covers, the wild duck are not so frequent in the bogs.   And so a long farewell to the moorlands, to Monarrogue, to Threenaheila-within-Drum, to Greenland! The sportsman who has graduated in these regions, and who has renewed his acquaintance with them, locks up his gun case and returns to town with a consciousness that there is not only health but a liberal education to be had by an interval of complete abandonment to wild-fowl shooting.

PICTURES FROM THE " WISP."

CHAPTER I.

AN OLD SPORTSMAN.

On the brown edge of Glenaugh Mountain my uncle Joe lived in the " Wisp." The Wisp was a stone mansion, with a small patch of garden in front, in which our henchman, Jack Sullivan, made certain experiments in horticulture, which, like many experiments in other pursuits, ended in nothing. Uncle Joe was a bachelor of small means, but was passionately addicted to shooting and fishing. These tastes he was in a great measure able to gratify, by acting as agent for a gentleman who owned most of the moorland and mountain in the district, and had the right of fishing in the river which flowed through the valley. Glenaugh was not an

inviting spot for a winter residence.   As far
almost as the eye could reach, nothing was to
be seen but a region of bog and heather.   The
heather stretched away up the mountain and
round its base, save where here and there white
and green reeds marked the treacherous morass.
But Uncle Joe cared not for poetical land-
scapes.   Glenaugh was a famous spot for game.
Many a night, when my uncle and I had our
guns brought up to the cosy parlour for in-
spection after cleaning by Jack Sullivan—many
a night have we paused at hearing, between
the shrill screams of the wind, the melancholy
piping of the plover, or the call of the mallard,
the whistle of the teal.   The heather gave
cover to great quantities of snipe and a fair
share of woodcock ; the bogs were literally full
of snipe.   Uncle Joe and I had the shooting
of the whole place to ourselves.   Our best
month decidedly was December.   There were,
strange to say, no grouse in the district ; and
although the snipe made their appearance in
October and November, still it was not until
the first touch of frost came that they were in
their prime, and in the largest numbers.   We

had some partridges in the few good farms of which the place could boast, but these we thinned off in a few weeks.

He was indeed a thorough sportsman, so far as shooting and fishing went. The den in the "Wisp" was completely devoted to implements of his craft. There was an armoury of small guns arranged round the walls. Fishing bags and nets were suspended from the ceiling. Pictures of wildfowl shooting and angling covered every available spot in the place. On the floor, by the wainscoat, were great regimental rows of boots and brogues. A favourite stuffed pointer in a glass case, and with very staring eyes, was hoisted on a bracket over the door, and the faded effigy of a bird near him was my uncle's first snipe. A bookcase in a corner contains many rare sporting treatises, for my uncle delights in the erudition of his pursuits. Above the chimney-piece is a map of the moors and fens and trout streams in the locality, carefully marked and coloured. There is a sort of MS. key or commentary to the chart in a private drawer, full of cunning hints as to the best days and hours and seasons for

E

freighting a bag or creel on the estate, and you should be deep in mine uncle's good graces indeed before he would lend you this precious concordance, which he values as highly as Parson Adams did his sermons.

These thin parchment-bound volumes—ten of them in all—are composed of pages profusely illustrated with flies. As an artificial entomologist my uncle was unparalleled. A tackle-maker once offered to name a wizard compound of feathers and fur which never failed to do its work on a salmon, after him, but my uncle was modest, and declined the proposed distinction.

Articles for cutting wads, manufacturing cartridges, bundles of bog whips, whistles, plover calls, quail pipes, gaffs, otter spears, and other litter of a similar kind are to be discovered in various crannies and angles of the shooting and fishing den.

Looking, the other day, into Macaulay's history, I noticed in one of the earlier chapters a curious account of the number of birds and wild animals that are now extinct, but which in the time of Charles II. were common enough throughout England. Referring to a footnote, I observed, quoted as an authority, 'The Gentleman's Recreation.' The dear old book was full, to me, of the pleasantest associations. It brought back the days of Christmas holidays, and that delightful holiday week with Uncle Joe at the "Wisp." His life was, indeed, made up of a round of shooting and fishing. He only put his gun in its case to take down his rod from the rack. On wet days he made artificial flies or cut wads. In fine weather, if the river or the season did not suit for actual sport, he had always a dog or so to break in, or would take a walk by the stream in order to mark where the biggest trout were feeding. Then there were his boots (he always prepared them himself) requiring to be anointed with a mysterious and evil-smelling compound, the recipe for which was taken from the veritable 'Gentleman's Recreation' above mentioned. Cleaning his gun at night in the kitchen was a tremendous business not at all popular with Molly, the cook, who would retire into a scullery to growl, while I held the jug of hot-water which Uncle Joe squirted with emphasis through the barrels, occasionally drenching a cat or a hen that might happen to be on the spot, in order to interest me more deeply in the proceedings. At the mature age of eight, I have trudged to a snipe bog with Uncle Joe, and being told by him to mark where a bird was to fall, have been caught with my eyes firmly closed in nervous expectance of the noise which, at first, had infinite terrors for me. I soon got over this, however, and well remember the time when, with the heavy old fowling-piece held to my shoulder by Uncle Joe, and directed by him (his finger pressing mine on the trigger), we, between us, compassed the death of a blackbird, which I subsequently insisted upon eating. After that I had a little single gun for myself, and committed havoc amongst starlings, sparrows, and such small fry. But Uncle Joe was constantly prompting me to nobler deeds. He held out a tempting reward for my first snipe. It was no less than Sill, a beautiful jet-black pointer. How I toiled to win this prize! We had plenty of marshes in the vicinity, and when Uncle Joe decided for a

day on the neighbouring mountains, his in-
structions to me were to go banging through
the bogs so as to flush the birds, which would
then pitch towards his beat. Nothing bothered
me more, at first, than the loud bleat of the
snipe as he sprang from the heather at my very
feet. I either did not fire at all, tugging at
half cock, or lodged the charge in the turf
about twelve yards from where I stood. But
my perseverance was finally rewarded. One
day I dropped, to my utmost astonishment, a
beautiful brown snipe; I ran like lightning to
pick him up, to the demoralization of an old
black retriever with whom I was entrusted.
Sill was mine, and from that time forward I
might, perhaps, hit three birds out of twenty.
I did not, for a considerable period, break
myself, however, of running at shot; as sure
as I saw the snipe fall I made a dash for him.
The consequence was ruinous to the character
of Sill the pointer, and Bob the retriever. At
first, those veterans were shy of imitating my
misconduct; but when they witnessed it four
or five times they joined in the sport, and it
was a race between us, Bob, Sill, and I, as to

who would be at the dead or wounded bird first. The sequel of this was, that I had to fight with them both for my game, and often came off with the worst share, Bob acquiring an appetite for raw snipe, which no subsequent flagellations on the part of my uncle could cure him of. I remember, indeed, that on his discovering our delinquencies (which he did when Sill and Bob, to his horror, made a dive and a grab into a covey of partridges), that he swore like the army in Flanders, and threatened to deprive me of all accoutrements if I did not, within one month, bring the dogs back to a sense of decorum. It was with some difficulty this was effected; the brutes had forgotten the commandments of " down shot " and " ware fence," and it was only by roaring myself hoarse and exercising a stoic vigilance over my own legs, that I reduced them once more to some kind of decent regard for the first principles of a shooting-dog's morality.

We did not confine our expeditions to the daytime. There were clear frosty nights in winter, when the stars sparkled, and you could hear the dreary calls of curlew or the thin pipe of a lone plover, sounding, as it were, quite close to you, although she might be miles up in the air. On such nights, Uncle Joe, having ascertained by the almanack that the moon would rise over the verge of the swamp at a favourable hour, would prepare for a raid on the wild duck. Muffled in thick coats, and accompanied by Jack Sullivan, my uncle's henchman, who bore pads of dry straw for us to sit upon, we wended our way to the moor. How silent and bleak it was, the pools shining here and there; and fishing by their edges, or sleeping on one leg, stood grey, ghastly herons. A snipe would occasionally start up, and sail like a hawk over our heads, or an owl would come sheering from somewhere out of the dark, his noiseless wings skimming the ground as he sought for a meal of field mice. But not for these did we come. Jumping across the dyke which divides the roadway from the marsh we now creep along the turf, softer than the softest pile carpet. "Hark! Down boys! down!" whispers Uncle Joe. A high querulous whistle, answered by a fat quack! quack! We all lie on our faces. There is a minute of dreadful suspense, during which I feel Di, my uncle's favourite and unfailing retriever, shuddering with excitement. At last, flop! as if out of the clouds drops a mallard into a pond close to us, and then another and another, and then, perhaps, a hundred, until the little patch of water is covered with them. "Will, you fire first," my uncle orders, a good deal under his breath.

I get ready at once, and aim for the centre of the birds. I have this time a double-barrelled gun. The light glints on the tubes, and with a mighty splashing, quacking, and whuttering, up start the ducks, but not before my uncle has sent three ounces of heavy shot amongst them, and I have also contributed to the slaughter. Eight or ten would be about the average number we picked up, and in the morning, Jack Sullivan would sally out and bring home, perhaps, three or four cripples.

If Uncle Joe was not shooting or fishing, or getting his implements in order for either of these pursuits, he was reading or talking about them. Hawker's 'Young Sportsman' and

'The Oakleigh Shooting Code' were the most modern works on fowling in his library; but he had a splendid collection of older worthies, such as good Nicholas Cox, Gentleman, author of 'The Gentleman's Recreation' before-mentioned. My uncle never tired of reading this latter treatise. It was full of the most quaint terms of language, and highly charged with that delicious enthusiasm in its subject, only to be found I think amongst our earliest sporting writers. It was, I remember, illustrated with a frontispiece, announced as " A Large Sculpture Giving Easie Directions for Blowing the Horne." Nor was Uncle Joe a mere ignorant game hunter. He studied the manners and habits of birds thoroughly; and it was a rare sight to see him stuffing any specimens that struck him as novel or peculiar. He had no fear of poachers, the "Wisp" being situated in a country where poachers are rare; and indeed, snipe shooting does not pay a poacher. My uncle never refused a day to any one applying to him, and the applicant was pretty sure of getting his dinner at the " Wisp " besides. It was a plain banquet enough, until the game

was put on, and then Uncle Joe triumphed.   I
verily believe that Francatelli was a fool to him
at sauces for teal, for woodcock, or for plover.
Father Brien, the priest of the parish, was a
frequent guest at our table; and his reverence
(who could bring down his brace right and
left as he walked across the moor to his little
chapel on week days) smacked his lips, I pro-
mise you, when the hot plates were laid on for
the birds.   He and Uncle Joe would com-
pare notes on the various beats of the district,
and strike out routes according to the relative
weight of the bags that had been made.

Between my uncle and myself there was the
strongest and most familiar intimacy that I
think ever existed between two persons in a
similar relation of life.   The fact is, that Joe,
from constantly living in the country, and
occupying himself solely with fishing and
shooting, or coursing, was as simple in the
ways of the world as a child; while I, save for
the periods of my vacations, had to subsist in
city fashion.   Joe, in truth, regarded me as
the older and more experienced of the two.   I
always looked forward to my visits to him for

unalloyed pleasure and keen enjoyment. He was the kindest soul in the world, and a dead shot. His agency business was a sinecure, inasmuch as a " driver" was kept to warn the tenants to go and pay their rents to a solicitor in the neighbouring county town ; and I believe that Joe's duties were never understood or settled, though the country people regarded him as the representative of the " master." So much was he liked that there never was a place better game-preserved than Glenaugh. The peasantry were poor and scattered ; but they never failed to send over to the Wisp to tell us if a string of duck had lodged on " Carty's ground," or that the plover were pitched in the widow Murphy's bawn-field. A glass of whisky was generally the reward for such intelligence as this, which was received as gravely by Jack Sullivan as though it related to the movements of an army, or a rising of the Fenians.

In December we got up in the morning, say at nine o'clock. During breakfast we discussed (with Mr. Sullivan, who was never absent from these cabinet councils) the route,

or, as we used to call it, the beat for the day.
A good deal would depend upon the weather
as to the direction to be taken.   For instance,
if it rained hard over night, the upper slopes of
the mountain would be patronized by whole
platoons of snipe from the bogs; if there was
a stiff frost, the lower lands and wet ditches
would be the quarters selected.   This is the
sort of scene that usually took place :

[*A small but snugly furnished room, with a
blazing turf fire on the hearth.   Uncle Joe, a
grizzled, open-countenanced veteran, as strong as
a horse, with a round bullet head and a clear
hazel eye, is demolishing eggs, for which he had
a huge appetite, with extraordinary gusto and
perseverance.   His nephew, the present writer, is
taking the post from Jack Sullivan, who' has
brought it from the gossoon despatched every day
to the village for letters.   Jack waits to get his
orders for the day.*]

   " Is it ' Flirt ' an' ' Don ' ye'll take out wid
ye, master ?"
   " No, Jack ; I think we'd better bring the
young bitch with old Don ; she wants to be

steadied. Did you hear of any cock ?" (wood-cock ; these birds are nearly always spoken of in Ireland without the indicative epithet).

" Callaghan says, yer honour, he put up a brace of 'em as he went gothern furze 'ere yesterday. 'Tis likely enough they are on the mountain now beein dhruv from the planta-tions be the fox-hounds that were huntin' there lately."

" Then how had we better go, Jack ? Master Willie wants as many shots at snipe as he can get."

" Well, sir, if we walks up Carty's ground fust, where the plover stand is, we may have a tech (touch) at them. I put up a hape of stones for stealin' on 'em a purpose. Thin, sir, Master Willie can bate for shnipes towards Callaghan's, while your honour might try the ould bawn-field at the end of Callaghan's hay-yard for the quails we saw there a Tuesday. We can meet thin, and I'll get some of the boys out wid sticks to try and knock up the cocks."

And so this plan of operations is probably adopted.

I should say here that my uncle Joe was so

far a genuine sportsman that he did not believe
in any shooting without the aid of a dog.

We never cared even to walk up snipe. Our
dogs were trained to examine the marshes as
cautiously as though they were travelling over
eggs ; and, strange to say, by judicious manage-
ment, this did not spoil them for wider ranges on
the mountain, when wide ranges were necessary.
We generally kept four dogs altogether ; a
brace of veterans and a couple of puppies in
their first or second season. Don, a huge setter,
so old that I should be afraid to give his age,
was our chief workman. Don was a most saga-
cious brute, as fond of shooting as we were
ourselves, enjoying it quite as much.   He
scorned to make mistakes.   He knew the
fields and quarters where we expected good
fortunes, at a glance, and would not be
bothered in searching those he put no faith in.
And we invariably trusted him.   My uncle
would as soon lay a whip on the back of the
faithful Sullivan as on the back of Don.   Flirt
was a brindled pointer, small, active, and rather
fidgety, with a nose so keen and nervous that
you could almost see the scent, as it were,

playing upon her quivering nostrils, when she came close upon her bird. The youngsters were not, of course, faultless; but in Uncle Joe's hands they either became so, or were dismissed our service. He hated flogging a dog. Flogging a dull stupid dog is quite as much a labour of supererogation, as Johnson would call it, as whipping a dull boy to make him clever.

A thin grey frost has fallen on the ground. The sky is blue and cloudless. Far off you see the saw-like edges of the Tipperary range, with that gap in the jaw of one hill which the devil is said to have made in a bite. The smoke from the cabins goes straight up into the air in a column like the rush of water from a fountain. The fields, the moors, are wonderfully, sadly still and silent; but we have come out to kill something. The dogs are already at work, for business opens at the immediate rear of the Wisp. My uncle, in his shooting-coat of many pockets, is inhaling draughts of the grand morning breeze, with a wonderful glow of satisfaction in his ripe cheeks. The dogs run back to him for a word of encourage-

ment or greeting now and then. Suddenly
Jack Sullivan calls out, " Whistsh," in a tone
of trembling entreaty. We halt. Uncle Joe
beckons to Don, but Don has become cataleptic,
and is beautifully backed by Flirt and a son of
hers worthy of his dam. From the nature of
the ground, we have little difficulty in guessing
that Jack has " sohoed " a hare in form.

At a sign from my uncle he advances and
pokes his stick into a bunch of heather. Out
pops poor luckless puss. A trying time this
for our four-footed friends, but they stand the
ordeal bravely. Don moves not a muscle ex-
cept to lay himself down with a sort of careless
grace, as though to indicate that his business,
so far, is over. There is just the slightest
quiver in the tail of the more impressionable
Flirt, while " Shot," the minor of the party,
behaves splendidly. I leave Uncle Joe the
honours of first blood. I never dream of
wiping his eye or expecting him to miss. No
flurry in *his* mode of raising his well-tried sub-
stantial Manton to his shoulder. The brown
tube rests for an instant as steady as a rock to
the level; the report rings out with a hard *thud*,

and the hare, with the full contents of the charge in the back of the head, rolls over and over again dead upon the heather. As we are so near the house, Jack, after the usual "More power to yer honour! a nate tidy shot!" runs into the kitchen with the prize, and Joe loads, and on we go again. There is great satisfaction in being successful in the first shot; it brings luck or the confidence that begets luck; but I have never known Uncle Joe to miss a hare but once, and that was only with the first barrel; the second barrel stopped her, though Joe was really astounded at having missed her at all. Here is a small patch of scrubby turnips that have been raised on this unkind soil with great difficulty. Joe proposes that I should try this for myself. He remains outside the low ditch, but full well I know that he is on full cock, and ready, on my failure, within seventy yards to have his turn at anything going. What is the matter with the dogs? Where are they? By Jove, lying *ventre à terre* in a furrow, stiff as though they were cut out of marble. I walk cautiously close to them. The sun is full in my eyes, but

F

cannot well alter my position now. I am a little nervous for a second as a fieldfare starts up; the dogs never stir. Nearer and nearer. Nothing moves. Nearer still—whir-r-r-r, and a large bird springs under my very nose into, as it seemed, the very disc of the sun. I fire quite blindly, dazzled with the light, but I hear the agreeable sound of a fall into the turnips, and a roar from Joe that he's dashed if it isn't one of Lord Gannin's pheasants. And so it was; and, I am sorry to say, a hen bird. A pheasant was a *rara avis* with us that we could not afford to let off. This bird had strayed in some manner from his lordship's preserves, about five miles from the spot. The nobleman was particularly stingy about his shooting, and neither Joe nor I were averse to taking an odd toll from the big stock of game it pleased him to keep up.

The day is so fine that the plover are not easy to approach. Far above us we can hear the querulous cry of the lapwing or green plover, but it is the golden plover we are after. While watching a white billow of mist which is born of the hoar frost from the valley, I note

a peculiar glint of wings in it, and with a warn-
ing to Uncle Joe and Jack, we all lie down in
the heather in profound silence. I keep my
eye fixed on the usual line of flight I know the
"stand" will take, and make a sign for Jack
to call. Jack can almost talk the unfortunate
plover near enough to have salt dropped on
their tails. He purses his mouth, and puts his
face towards the ground, and a wonderfully
clear tone and semitone travel into the frosty
atmosphere. We listen earnestly. Hark!
the answer is returned. Again Jack performs,
and again the vanguard of the plover brigade
responds to him—this time in a quick and
eager style. And now, rushing towards us
right from a straight line, and covering an
extent of five or six hundred yards, we see the
birds. Jack's lure has been almost too per-
fect, for as they are preparing to alight they
spread themselves out, and we can only get a
front shot at them. They are drawing quite
close, but from the mode of their advance it
would be impossible to do much execution,
and so we execute the following manœuvre :
when the plover are about thirty yards from

us we jump to our feet, when the whole flock
suddenly falls into rank, and sheers off like
lightning in a sort of close column. *Bang,
bang, bang, bang!* a whole cloud of feathers
and a goodly number of the delicious fowl (I
prefer them to any of our wild-fowl, save teal,
for the table) are tumbled over, while odd
cripples are dropping out of the scurrying but
silent army that now plunges nervously over
the tops of the heather, anon tosses itself as
though with the single impulse far up into the
air.   Five brace altogether, Jack Sullivan
gathers, and opines from our commencement
that we'll have what he calls "a good day av
it."   Approaching   the   residence   of   Mr.
Callaghan, farmer and tailor.   Mr. Callaghan
lives in a mud edifice pleasantly placed in a
bog.   This is literally true, although it is a
poetic quotation.   There is a pretty green cess-
pool before the hall-door, on the sill of which
a pig is talking to himself.   A few ducks are
studying the contents of a pile of rubbish
which ornaments the south bank of the mere
aforesaid.   A ramshackle cowhouse, and out-
side it the *boreen* (lane), over the stone wall of

which a man in a flannel jacket is looking at us. This is Mr. Callaghan, one of the greatest idlers and best-natured ne'er-do-weels I ever met amongst the Irish peasantry. He visibly brightens as he sees us ; he will walk with us all day " to show his honour the birds," and so excuse himself for not finishing his drains or the Sunday coat he has promised to make for the parish clerk of Glenaugh.

" Mornin', gintlemen, mornin' t'ye ! Did ye do much ?"

" Pretty well, Tim. We. heard you saw some cock about here."

" Yis, sir ; I put up a brace o' 'em over foreninst the strame. Maybe yer honners would come in and take a sate while I get my *kipeen* (stick) to bate the *broshna* (furze)."

(Enter the Casa Callaghana).

The smoke and stuffiness of the place is dreadful. A young comely woman, the lady of the house, greets us, and takes off the floor out of the way a curly-pated beautiful young Celt, smirched with the gutter confection which he has been manufacturing since he got up at cockcrow. The room has no ceiling: you see the black rafters and the rotten thatch gloom over your head. There is a second apartment, in which the family retire (into one bed) for the night. At present the Callaghans are not overcrowded, comprehending only Mr. and Mrs. Callaghan and the *gossoon*, or heir. Tim Callaghan is supposed, by his neighbours, to be snug, and with all this air of slatternly discomfort you note that none of the lot seem either hungry or dissatisfied. Tim respectfully produces a black bottle, and wants to know " av he might make bould to offer us a drop of the cratur," but we decline, and the kipeen (a stout blackthorn) being produced from the back of the dresser on which the crockery of the establishment is displayed, we march out for our raid upon the " cocks." We have to cross a brawling swollen brook on stepping-stones, and landing on the other side find ourselves at the base of a rather high and steep hill, covered with thick thorny furze, in which it is extremely difficult to walk. We are here compelled to leave the dogs below, as their feet and tails would be sadly torn in this spot. As it is, although I am well shod and gaitered, at times I receive a flesh-wound that causes me to jerk uneasily; and as we are obliged to carry our guns on ready, and follow Jack and Tim, who are respectively below and above us, the situation is not quite as secure or as pleasurable as it might be. Our servitors are making a hideous uproar, considering that there are only two of them. *Hie, cock, cock, cock ! Hie, cock, cock, cock ;* then *thwack, thwack* against the bushes. Mark ! The bird starts up at Joe's side, and flies over the stream swift as a shadow. My uncle has his wrong leg first, and bringing up his gun gets into a kind of knot, and misses.

" O blood alive, master," roars Jack, " he's off, the bligard !"

" Well, we can't hit everything, Jack," returns my uncle good-humouredly, though I see from his face that he is a little mortified at his disaster.

" There's another here, sir, I'm shure," remarks Mr. Callaghan ; but he was wrong in his conjecture, or, at least, the bird was wise enough not to make his appearance, for we beat the entire of the cover in vain, and then prepared for a razzia into a long string of bogs, which we agreed to divide between us. My uncle was to take Jack Sullivan and one side of it with Flirt; I was to take the other with Don, Shot, and Tim Callaghan, who had now attached himself to us for the remainder of our expedition. At this point we all observe a deep silence, for, strange enough, snipe or even wild duck will not start from a bog at the sound of a gun as readily as they will either at the sound of a voice, the noise of the feet sinking in the slush, or the whutter made by their own wings. Uncle Joe and I both draw our charges (we are unfashionable enough to shoot with muzzle-loaders), and substitute number eight for number six; and then Joe takes the left circuit, while I take the right. The place is hot with scent, and the dogs are cowering and stealing prettily about us. Don first stops, and as we are at present close to each, is backed by the others. A jack skirls like a dark butterfly in a breeze, waggling in a most bewildering style, but Joe waits until his flight has attained his climacteric, and while the jack is poised for one second, he leaves his life in the air, and flops into a small pool a dozen yards off.

"*Mark!* sir, *mark!*" says Callaghan, in a low eager tone to me; and, alas! ten yards, at least, out of range, ten splendid mountain duck skim along swift as partridges, and then dart aloft and wheel and wheel higher and higher until they fall backwards to "Shanabogue, bad luck to 'em," Mr. Callaghan opines. Here we shot a teal and three water hens, besides ten brace of snipe, between us. When we met at the point of junction, we sat down in the heather, lit our pipes, drank a stoup of water with a dash of spirits in it, and concerted our next move.

"There's a covey of pitteridges on Carey's land, av ye'd like to after 'em, gintlemen," remarks Mr. Callaghan. But this proposition is received with disfavour. Our wish is to make as big a bag of snipe as possible; and, as many of those we have sprung may lie on the wet mountain, we once more shoulder our guns, and take to the limitless brown slopes. The cover here between the withered fern, the heather, stray patches of rush, and shallow pools of water with rich black ooze on their edges, make a splendid resort for game. Mr. Callaghan is haunted with a notion that cocks make up the chief fun of a sportsman, and he is never wearied thrashing for these birds. We got a couple of them before we had put a mile behind us and our resting-place; but the snipe were rather wild, as they always are after a grey frost. And now the day begins to die; and as the sun sinks, great banks of mist creep in around us, and there is a chill damp in the air presaging rain. The dogs, too, are wearied and a bit footsore, for this mountain work tells on them, and carries out my pet theory that both pointers and setters ought to be shod. Yet the willing brutes hold out bravely at a word and gesture of encouragement from Uncle Joe, who cheers them to the beat from time to time, and who is himself as fresh as when he started. The rain, however, begins to come on in earnest in an hour, when indeed our bags are very reasonably full; and I have quite enough for consumption at the Wisp and for importation to town, to which I have faithfully promised to despatch some snipe. At length we call a halt, and face the Wisp. The rain is not thick, but cold enough to touch the marrow of the bone. The dreary desolate moorside seems to close in upon us; and already the curlew, who seldom speak until the dusk, are conversing to each other in the dim shadows overhead. We have had such a good day that Mr. Callaghan, who bears my bag, while Sullivan carries Joe's, is indulging in a song. He has a queer ring in his voice—a melancholy whine running through a vein of fun, which you may have heard Mr. Boucicault or poor Charles Verner imitate not badly. The words of his ditty are in Gaelic, and do not sound as softly as Italian.

A red glint two miles from here—a glint that comes and goes like a revolving light at sea—that is the Wisp. Uncle Joe and I are both silent. The fact is, we brought no sandwiches with us, and are both so hungry that we can think of nothing but our dinners. The worst of it is, that a hungry man's stomach seems to delight in tantalizing his imagination, and through it his palate, at such a moment. As I shamble by my uncle's side in the mirk, heavy-footed now, I can tell you I remember having heard that there was a cod's-head and oyster-sauce, a small leg of mutton, and game *ad libitum* for dinner. I keep revolving these good things in my head until I have doubts on the subject of the cod's-head.

" Uncle Joe, are we to have the cod's-head to-day ?"

Joe looks at me reproachfully. The poor man himself is as famished as a hawk in a a parish of sparrow-shooters, and I feel that my question is little short of indecent.

" I'm horribly hungry, Will," he says, and puts on a fresh spurt.

We put the dogs into the kitchen, to dry and snooze before the hearth until a snug mess is got ready for them. And oh ! the luxury of dry clothes, of slippers, of a glass of sound clean sherry before——before that cod's-head makes its welcome appearance.

The shots are duly discussed——the misses, why they were missed; the hits, how cleverly they were pulled off. The cheery fire grows cheerier. Hark ! a wind rises on the hill and tears round the Wisp with a sharp whish——but what care we for winter or foul weather with this roof over our heads, and pipes and ale, or Kinahan or wine, what you will, until we are ready to lie between the white sheets and sleep the dreamless sleep of the wearied sportsman ?

However, I am unable now to sketch an evening at the Wisp as it ought to be done. The night I refer to we did not leave his reverence to depart, but we sent Jack Sullivan across to his dwelling to mention his whereabouts in case of an urgent sick-call. And the hours went on with stories, with depletion of tumblers, with lighting of cigars, with tunes by my Uncle Joe on the violin, on which instrument he was an accomplished player.

CHAPTER II.

MEMORIES OF GLENAUGH.

I MIGHT, if I would, indite this with a feather plucked from a mallard shot within a perch of the parlour window, even as Robin Hood brought a quill from a goose in the sky with an arrow from his unerring bow. I am surrounded with guns and dogs, and with trophies of Uncle Joe's deeds with his Manton. There, over the chimney-piece, is the famous solitary snipe bagged in Murphy's bogs. Next to the solitary snipe is our bittern, slain by Jack Sullivan with a shillelagh as it darted from a bunch of reeds. In a case next to it you will perceive Flirt, the last of a breed of pointers known as the button-tailed, and which were, in truth, as destitute of natural rudders as the Manx cats. My uncle was an excellent judge of dogs, and a capital trainer; but I have not been either as fortunate or perhaps so skilful. Perhaps a few of my experiences may serve to amuse the reader.

I believe every dog has a character as distinctive and as marked as that of a man or a woman, and not only are the characteristics apparent, but at times dogs exhibit a curious individuality of temperament. There are odd dogs as well as odd people, and I think my pointer Sam was the oddest brute that ever wagged a tail.

I purchased him for thirty shillings from a

gaunt peasant, who disappeared so quickly the moment I paid him that it struck me his version of how Sam came into his hands was open to doubt. However, I did not dwell much on this, and as I took my acquisition downstairs to give him supper I felt highly gratified with my bargain. A coal-black pointer is not common, and Sam was as black as a conscientious nigger melodist. He was of great size, and about three years old. I brought him out early next morning along with a small retrieving spaniel. There was a slight moisture in the turnips and stubble, and Sam (who quartered and beat about his ground in excellent style) to my surprise began gradually, as it were, to grow pale all over. I called him to heel, and passed my hand down his coat, when lo! I found that the poor animal had been as carefully black-leaded as an ornamental grate, and that the stuff was coming off with the wet. I made him swim in a dyke, and when he rolled and shook himself after it he discovered his real quality or suit, white and brown, and I was glad to observe that he did not alter his complexion again in the course of the day.

He was a splendid dog to work, but I soon discovered that he would do nothing, positively nothing, if I brought any other assistant with me. He growled at the little spaniel audibly, even at their first meeting, and ever afterwards used to run back into the yard if he saw me attended by one of the other dogs. Another peculiarity of Sam's was that he was as sure as fate to run away from a bad shot. I have lent him out to some tyros, who had permission from me to try their hands at snipe close in the neighbourhood, and have been intensely amused when, after an hour's banging in the bog, Mr. Green would come up and complain that Sam had disappeared. "Come now," I would say, "you must have been unlucky. Have you much in the bag?" The answer was invariably, "No; a little nervous," etc. etc. Sam at this time was certain to be found snugly before the kitchen fire, knocking his tail against the flooring, as if indignant at the poor shooting he had witnessed.

He had a perfect nose, had Sam, and a happy knack of indicating the sort of game he pointed. This was exceedingly useful in an open country and on heath, where you never could tell whether snipe, cock, a hare, or partridge might be about or not. Sam had his own way of approaching each. His only vice was a strong taste for hare. I had to correct him for this, and it was pitiable afterwards to observe his wistful look at a retreating puss, and the convulsive action of his jaws, as if he were turning over an imaginary piece in his mouth. His instinct for detecting jack snipe was exceedingly troublesome. He far preferred drawing on a jack to finding the hottest covey of partridge, and would often lead me away from larger game in order to poke out his enemy, and he was never satisfied until the jack was bagged. I have seen him positively give a caper (which I ascribe to sheer delight) when, after missing the little beggar a couple of shots, I have brought him down with a third.

Madge was another eccentric pointer. Madge was a lady, but a lady with a deuce of a temper, and (a most unusual thing with such dogs) a perfect glutton to fight. Woe betide the terrier who barked from the farmhouse near which she passed. On the instant she was into his wool, and if he had companions she seemed to relish the combat all the better. I recollect once being warned off certain lands by a keeper. Madge flew at him as if she knew the nature of his remonstrance, and it was with some trouble I whipped her into propriety. I recollect again passing soldiers on the march. There was a small dog in front of the detachment who gave a sort of defiant yelp at Madge. The next thing I saw was Madge charging sideways into the front rank of the soldiers, knocking two of them at least out of step, and collaring the now squealing offender. Of course this was inconvenient for me. I had had more than once to pay for injuries done to pets and to the trousers or skins, as it might happen, of the people in my vicinity. Yet Madge was worth the expense. She had wonderful go in her, and could stand anything but the frost.

Tom was presented to me by a famous breeder. I expected great things from him. He turned out a perfect fool. I had almost written ass, but for the confusion involved in

the comparison. Still, to paraphrase an ac-
count of another animal in ' Tristram Shandy,'
he went through his performances with such a
gravity of demeanour that you were constantly
sold by him. He would trot in a solemn, wise
manner into a field, put his head up in good
style to sniff the scent, look round and invite
you to follow; get gradually, as it were, more
anxious, until at length he stood steady as a
rock pointing at nothing. You might forgive
him if birds had been there, but as a rule Tom
would just as soon as not put you through the
above figures without the slightest, the scantiest
grounds for his exhibition. I once saw him
come to a dead point on an asphalte pavement,
where there wasn't even a blue-bottle. He was
beautiful to look at, and evidently proud of his
proportions. He would give his life for a piece
of sweet cake, and would follow children about,
doing everything but asking for some, half the
day. When he was in good luck he always
spent a long time over the morsel, and I
suspect that his mind was so demoralized by
confectionery that he was unable to bring it to
bear upon his business. He was an utter dis-

grace to his father and mother, his brothers,
sisters, and his cousins, all of whom had been
more or less distinguished. I had a grave
suspicion once that he bolted an entire snipe
behind my back, while pretending to "find
dead." Unless the bird dropped through the
ground I don't know how else to understand
my not procuring it, but the notion involves
an amount of cunning on the part of Tom for
which I wouldn't give him credit. Yet your
fool is sometimes a knave also. A friend of
mine asked me for the loan of Tom for a
month. He told me afterwards he never met
such a "pointer," nor so bad a "finder." He
pointed everything and everywhere. He was
discovered "pointing" a child's shoe on a gar-
den walk, and having a similar rehearsal over a
raw potato in a scullery. His attitude in these
cases was all that could be desired, but attitude
is not all that is wanting in the field. Tom has
stood for his portrait, and you would swear by
the impostor unless you had experience of him.
I never had the heart to beat him for his stu-
pidity ; it appeared so hopeless and so comical.
He had an intense affection for his master, and

although that may be considered an additional proof of his dull powers of perception it covered with me a multitude of faults.

, I have not yet exhausted my list of eccentric pointers. Don I never could break from chasing cows and baying the moon, whenever he saw it, or a glimpse of it. Nor would he eat, no matter how hungry, if any one was looking at him. I have tested him severely in this respect, but he held out until my patience was exhausted. I have had dogs that all the training in the world could not break from running at particular birds, and others who from puppies seemed to have been thoroughly educated. I had a pointer who never would swim a drain, who would run round miles sooner than cross a shallow brook. I had another who was an incorrigible thief of the magpie order. His name was Peter. Peter was afflicted with kleptomania late in life, and the attacks were frequent and of great severity. He stole spoons and knives and forks as deftly as a pickpocket or burglar christian. He would hide them in his straw. For what purpose? I never could make out. Certainly not to eat his meals with.

He came by a horrible death. His evil pro-
pensities were the cause of it; a stolen box of
matches the Nemesis. He hid away the box,
and must have been striking a light or amusing
himself in some manner with it during the
night; anyhow the matches took fire, and
Peter was burned to such an extent that I
had to end his sufferings by shooting him.
Long after his premature demise missing
things were found in various corners of the
stables and outhouses. I was sorry for Peter,
for though ageing and slow of gait, a better
dog on snipe I never brought up, and in his
youth he was very fair as a general practi-
tioner.

My private impression is that many of these
pointers were humourists, with a great deal of
undeveloped comedy in them. A dog has few
opportunities for being witty, but then he has
a chance now and again of amusing himself at
your expense, and I believe pointers are a race
peculiarly gifted in this respect.

But to return to the 'Wisp.' On my ar-
rival a few weeks back we had prime sport at
both cock and snipe. The cock were plen-

tiful; and we did badly if we did not bring home thirteen or fourteen brace of snipe. For all this I never met such a grumbler as Jack Sullivan. He is the most incorrigible growler. "The birds is lavin' the country," he says bitterly; "and what else are ye to expict from the state 'tis in?" Also, "They're not half the size they wor; an' as for the cocks, they're nothin' but *thraneens*" (tit-larks) "kimpared wud the cocks av ould times." Joe, however, who never intends to grow old, is as cautious as Swift was to avoid the usual symptoms of that inevitable condition. He is careful not to prose or to maunder about epochs that are to me as the dark ages, and he is satisfied with the bags we pick up; his pedestrian powers are yet amazing—in fact, no amount of exertion seems to tire him. Occasionally I used to drive off some five or six miles towards the coast for an evening's shooting at the Pill. Uncle Joe seldom cared to accompany me on these expeditions.

The Pill is a creek with mud banks up which birds that haunt the sea come at certain times of wind and tide. It was a great resource to

me on days when I did not care to beat the
heather for snipe. I was confident of some
shooting there, and the most agreeable feature
about the sport was the uncertainty of what
you could pick up. In wild weather, when the
wind roared and whistled in froin the white
breakers under the grey sky, great flocks of
plover wheeled up the creek, and gave me
many a chance of a broadside. There was no
necessity for a boat. The banks were close
together, and with the aid of a stout retriever
and the fortune of the birds tumbling on the
ground instead of the water, losses from acci-
dent were very few. An old barn stood on one
edge of the Pill. Behind the broken wall of
this, and commanding the passage which the
red shank, widgeon, or plover generally took,
I used to place myself. It was often quick and
hot work enough, especially with an east or a
north gale. On such occasions I always ex-
pected better fun than usual. During calm
days the best bags were to be made of curlew
(a poor bird on a dish no matter what may be
said for it), and a bird that I called a sea pie,
though I am not sure whether that is the cor-

rect term or not. It was capital when served on toast.

I am now going to tell you how I saw the devil at the Pill. It isn't often we see the devil out of the opera, and when a sportsman falls in with black game of so quaint a kind he is bound to record it. I had been dining with a friend in the neighbourhood, who had excellent stories, capital whisky, or claret if you preferred it, and a keen Irish sense of fun. When we had disposed of the repast, to us enters Tim Dennehy, ostler, greyhound trainer, and handy man in general to the establishment.

" Cold night, Tim."

" Yis, Sir, could it is." (*Tim looked at the decanter. His master poured out a glass. Tim took it in hand, and it seemed to disappear down his sleeve, I think, so unconscious did his face appear of having swallowed it.*)

" How's the tide, Tim ?"

" An ould man, yer honour " (high-water, on the point of going out).

" Would the gentleman have a chance of getting at the duck, do you think ?"

" Musha thin, 'tis hard to say, Sir.   They're yawry (wary) craturs thim ducks, but it wud be no harm af he was after tryin'."

" I should desire nothing better," said I, getting up.   My host, I knew, had some duties to perform in the neighbourhood, and I took my gun from the hall rack and sallied out for the Pill.

Ugh ! it was a cold night.   The wind nipped one's ears as if a bad barber was cutting one's hair and a little skin with it.   The Pill was close by, and in the moonlight the wet banks from which the sea had subsided looked like mounds of silver.   The air was crisp and thin with frost, and you could hear the tide snoring outside in the dark, while the calls of the various birds fell all round quaintly and even musically.

I got behind the barn and watched the mouth of the creek narrowly.   Four curlews dart up, followed by a string of red shank.   A belated gull flaps heavily along, after him a cormorant swift as an arrow, and skimming the surface of the water.   As yet there is no sign of the duck.   I can hear them, however, plain

enough, and bide my time. I light my pipe.
There is nothing like tobacco in such a situa-
tion. I was well muffled up, and had capital
shelter from the wall of the barn. As I smoked
somehow or other I felt drowsy. I nodded
(only two tumblers on my honour, only two.)
I pulled myself together. I nodded again—it
was all—a noddin—nid, nid noddin—all a—
Hallo !

I rubbed my eyes, as they say in stories (this
is no story, this is truth, Messieurs), there could
be no doubt of it, none whatever! There he
was. There, stealing down the bank, horns
and all !

The horns did it. I might have argued my-
self out of my fears, but for those appendages.
Horns are a monopoly of the ——— nowadays.
The ——— moved in a line with me, and then
towards me. I had no charmed bullets, no
magic sixpences, and somehow I thought a
charge of duck shot, or of Eley's wire car-
tridge No. 4, would be too much even for
the ——— at point blank (especially if I made
a mistake). So having an easy conscience, I
waited. Nearer and nearer the figure came,

until when within twenty yards the —— called out in the voice and the brogue of Tim Dinnehy, "Where are ye, Sir?" .... Tim had been sent down to help me home—with the birds. His horns had arisen from his having tied a handkerchief round his head in place of a hat, and the ends stuck over his ears in the diabolical fashion, as may be seen in the illustrations to the 'Ingoldsby Legends.'

In frosty weather I have shot splendid bags of birds at the Pill. Even snipe resorted to it, flying up and down here when the marshes were icebound. You required to be warmly cased for this work, and to bring heavy shot. It was also necessary to get into the habit of firing a long way before the birds, as they mostly came with a spurt through the creek, which led to a large shallow.

One more story of the Pill before I close. There lived a man near it, the landlord of a shebeen, from whom refreshments could be procured. The hotel was thatched, and in constant want of repairs. On a certain occasion I was accompanied by a Cockney friend, and we went up to Mr. Ryan's establishment for man and horse. Mr. Ryan was on the roof smoking and mending the thatch.

"Good morrow, yer honour," said Mr. Ryan.

"Good morrow, Mick," I replied.

"D'ye want a drop, gentlemen?"

"Yes," I answered. Whereupon Mr. Ryan, to my friend's intense astonishment (I had seen the feat performed before), slided down the roof of his house with the greatest nonchalance, and proceeded to introduce us to the hospitalities of it.

Did I say that besides the ubiquitous and Briarean Sullivan we retain an ancient servitor in the kitchen who can do plain cooking to perfection? The only fault Molly has is her temper; but "God help us," remarks Mr. Sullivan, "that's the divil entirely." Molly constantly gives warning, and bemoans the fate that has condemned her to the ' Wisp ' in periodical spasms of misanthropy. During these intervals she says "she never sees the face av a Christian only whin the priest comes to the house ; an' what wid sportin' an' gallivantin' 'an dhrinkin' punch, she wonders the roof doesn't

fall upon our heads." She soon recovers her-
self from these fits, which are brought to a
crisis by the figure of Jack Sullivan with a
pipe in his mouth at the corner of the hob
paying not the least attention to the explo-
sions. "Yerra, woman, why don't ye be aisy?
Shure 'tis little to do ye have after all, an' ye
might go farther an' fare worse." Now it was
a peculiarity of Molly's, that, no matter how
cross she might be, she never failed in having
the dinner duly on the table; and, indeed, she
confined her tantrums entirely to rhetorical and
sentimental assertions of grievances. I won
her heart by a judicious present of snuff. I
brought her as much "sneeshin'" as would fill
the Mull of Cantyre (whatever that is), and a
box for carrying charges of the brown stuff of
a solid, if not very expensive, manufacture.

For the last two days we have been con-
fined closely to the Wisp by the weather.
The 'whish' of the rain has never ceased for a
moment, and shooting has been out of the
question. We consult the glass (the baro-
metrical glass), and we summon Mr. Sullivan,
who runs to the back door, gazes mournfully

up the sides of Glenaugh, and comes back to say he's "afraid 'tis thickenin' in the clear." This is an involved expression, which means that in that particular quarter of the heavens from which hope of truce might be held out there was no longer that promise. What is to be done?

My uncle takes down his fly-book and a box holding all sorts of stuff for the making of the lures by which the silver salmon or the golden trout are brought to the bank. For a while I am sufficiently amused examining the various odds and ends which this box holds. In one corner of it is a wonderful bottle which must not be lightly spoken of. The liquid in the phial is almost as precious as the elixir of life. You might guess for ever without hitting off its use. It is only to true believers .that Joe reveals the secrets of the mixture. It is intended for nothing less than the generation of worms. Joe swears that it accelerates the ordinary process, and has also the effect of rendering the bait tough and lively. I would not advise any naturalist or chemist to contradict him.

"Take a look-out, Will, and see if there is any chance of the day mending."

What a prospect! The ground sodden and black, the rain clouds in ragged skirts trailing across the valley, no sign of man or cattle or life of any sort upon the desolate dismal landscape. I turn in with a sense of comfort to the snug parlour, and, for want of a job, endeavour to cobble together the torn meshes of a game-bag. My uncle is so absorbed just now with the dressing of a Limerick hook, that to interrupt him would be trying even to his excellent temper. Shall I, for a change, shift my quarters to the kitchen? Molly places a stool for me by the ample fireplace. Jack Sullivan sits opposite plucking a wild-duck. Every moment a heavy drop of rain splashes from the cavern of the chimney upon the glowing turf. There is a battered relict of the turnspit race fast asleep on the ground. The ceiling is hung with huge slabs of bacon, and indeed we are well provisioned against a siege at the Wisp. Some such thought as this suggests my asking Mr. Sullivan what he thinks of the Fenian movement.

" Idle bligards, the lot of 'em!" remarks
Mr. Sullivan. " I didn't care av they wor
transported, every mother's son of 'em. Isn't
it bekaise they won't do a stroke of work or
strive to airn an honest——"

" Yerra, hould yer tongue, ye omadhaun,"
breaks in Molly. " It well becomes the likes
a you to talk agin thim that wants to free the
country."

I press an explanation on the phrase " free-
ing the country."

" Musha, thin, sir, shur what wid sojers and
peelers we're ate up complately, and there's
nothing for a poor man, or a poor woman
ayther, but to gother what they have an' take
it wid 'em to Americay."

" Baithershin," replies Mr. Sullivan, " an'
why don't you go to Americay?"

Molly does not condescend to give a re-
sponse to this suggestion, and the political
debate drops dead, nobody caring to resume it.

Still the rain, the rain, as if there were an
ocean emptied upon us. It is as yet only two
o'clock.

I make a sudden resolve. Why not test

H

my waterproof coat, my famous boots anointed with the impervious unguent, during the next couple of hours ?   Joe thinks I am mad as I envelop myself in these startling wrappers, and, with loaded gun, sally up the steep of Glenaugh.

Jack Sullivan gazes after me speechless with surprise at my foolhardiness.

The first dash into the wet was pleasant enough. The wind and rain smiting me full in the face caused me to put one shoulder forward, as it were, to meet the next buffet.   I scarce expected to have a shot—indeed, it was almost impossible to see beyond a distance of twenty yards.

Hark !   The call of a golden plover almost at my ear.   I glance round; there is no sign of the bird; but again the querulous pipe sounds, and this time I look up and see a single plover wheeling a few feet above my head.

The gun gives out a short dull report, and the smoke hangs round the muzzle like a grey veil, when I pick up the strayed wanderer. Perhaps the stand is in the neighbourhood.

I catch the squeak of the snipe as they jerk themselves from the heather, but find it out of the question to cover one of them; the rain falls still harder and faster and colder.

To keep myself warm, I walk quicker. I begin to sing too, the wind occasionally snapping the notes from my mouth, or sending the air into wild incoherent intervals.

Already the Wisp is completely hidden by the mist, though I am sure I know the exact direction in which it lies; and so I bend my steps towards it. The slope is in my favour, and I bowl along merrily, thinking of the cheery evening before me, to which a zest has been given by this little voluntary hardship. I trot down the decline for half an hour and more. It is now dark, pitch dark: surely the Wisp should be close at hand? And sure enough—"Hallo, Jack! house a-hoy!"

Eh, what's this? A man with a lantern, who jumps over a wall I had not perceived before. Callaghan the tailor hight is he.

"Is that you, Master Will? Yerra, thin, sir, isn't it an awful night for ye to be out?"

"I thought I was at my uncle's, at the Wisp,

Tim; but it appears I must have lost my way." (I had, by at least two miles.)

"Come in, sir, and take a hate av the fire; and thin I'll walk across wid yer honour."

I decline Tim's hospitality, but not his guidance. Tim is nothing loth to do suit and service on such occasions, as he experiences the pleasures of a gossip with Molly and Sullivan, besides sundry convivial jorums partaken of in their society in the comfortable kitchen of the Wisp.

"I was getting a little anxious about you, Will," said my uncle, as I came from my bed-room after dressing for dinner by putting on an old suit of clothes and a pair of slippers. "I was on the point of despatching Jack to look for you on the mountain; but I hesitated before doing that, as, if you happened to call out suddenly in the dark, the fellow would have fainted with fright."

"How's that? I thought Jack was as stout-hearted as a lion."

"And so he is, but as superstitious as a negro. He is a firm believer in ghosts; at least in one ghost. I am surprised he never told you the story."

"Never. We'll have him up after dinner. This is just the night for a ghost story."

"Ay; and I promise you Jack's apparition is as original as Jack himself."

"But do you think there will be any trouble in drawing him out?"

"Leave that to me. Is Tim Callaghan below?"

"Yes."

"So much the better; Tim will be of use."

And so it is decided that we are to extract from Jack Sullivan the great story—the story of an event which has, at any rate, seriously injured his nerves. When the cloth was off, my uncle asked Molly to send up the two boys.

Tim Callaghan is the first to enter with a rustic shuffle upon the rug.

"Good-evenin', Tim."

"Good-evenin' to your honour."

"Tim, I hope you settled that affair between yourself and Shaun Webb. You know, I don't want ye to be taking the law of each other."

"An' what am I to do, sir? Only to-day

mornin' we found the bottom full o' the flood, after his promise to yer honour to keep it dry."

"Well, Tim, we won't bother about it now. Here's a tumbler of punch for you.—Jack!"

"Yes, yer honour."

"Master Will wants to hear how you saw the ghost of Donogh Freney. Sit down, both of you, on the sofa there; and, Jack, commence at once. Here's something to keep your voice from growing husky."

"Long life to you, master! An', av you plase, I'll tell the narrashin."

As Jack got himself into an attitude for this purpose, Molly stole to the open door, and at a gesture from my uncle came into the room, where she leaned against the wall, forming one of the audience.

"Well, sir," commenced Jack, addressing himself directly to me, "you must know that Donogh Freney was iver and always a bad boy. He'd curse his own father an' mother, and throw stones at the beggars. When a bit of a fight tuk place at a fair or a patthern, he was the fust to commence an' the last to lave off; an' if a wicked sthroke was given, 'twas sure to be by Donogh Dhuv, as he was called, by raison of his black hair an' his black looks. Often and often the priest warned him of his evil doin's; but Donogh only grinned at his reverence, an' could never be got by the same token to attind to his duty. His poor wife, the cratur, had a bitter lot in store for herself by him. He dhrank whatever he airned; an' only for the naybors, God knows but there never would be a bit or sup in the house to keep starvashin from the door. She came of dacent people, the Murphys of Ballycasey; and at long last, when Donogh Dhuv put the welt of a stick on her face, she ran away from him to her father. Her brother, Tom Murphy, widout sayin' a word, came up to Mr. Boyce's haggard, where Donogh was at work be himself. What passed betune thim first never was known; but anyhow, Donogh was found killed wid a pitchfork in the haggard, and Tom Murphy went off wid his sister to Americay, and never has been heard of from that day to this.

"About three years after, I was doin' a bit

of a job for Mr. Joyce; and when it was over, I come in and sat in the kitchen just as it might be, sir, savin' your presence, here, waitin' until it was time for me to walk home. I lit my pipe, an' I suddenly remimbered that I had left my ould caubeen in the haggard. So, widout thinkin' a nothin', I opens the door ladin' to the yard. The night was dark, but there was a strake o' moonlight near the fut of a ladder close to the haggard; an', to me surprise, I see Bill Walshe, who minded the pigs an' things, stoopin' down close by this. 'Bill,' says I, 'there's a caubeen o' mine foremust the haggard; will ye bring it in wid you when you're comin'?' The never a word from Bill. 'Begor,' says I to myself, 'this is a quare business.' An' wid that, sir, I walks up to the spot, an' my heart was in my mouth, when, as if it melted, the figure at the end of the ladder wint away. I caught hold av my hat, an' was runnin' in as fast as my legs could carry me, when somethin', I dunna what, made me look round again; an' there, sure enough, was that same that I took for Bill Walshe, stoopin' down just as I saw it afore. 'In God's name,'

I says, 'who are you?' Up laped the ghost, for ghost it was, wid the ugly scowl of Donogh Dhuv on its face; and at the moment I lost my sinses, until I recovered, when I found myself in the kitchen. I'm not the same man since, Master Will, an' never expect to be; for to my dyin' day I never can put out of my head the thoughts of the sperrit of Donogh, who came be his end without clargy or sacrament."

After the story, Molly, Jack, and Tim took their departure, Tim receiving orders from my uncle to be in readiness next morning with Jack to help us in beating, if the day were favourable for sport.

The weather was better the following morning. As the previous night had been so wet we agreed to try the heather first for the snipe. Although we found the birds a little wild, we had capital sport.; and by twelve o'clock (having commenced at ten) we need not have been ashamed to turn out our bags before Colonel Háwker himself. After this we made a detour of the bogs, and got a couple of hares and four brace of wild duck. We were unable, however, to come at the plover, in consequence of a number of lapwing mixing with them, and rendering them unapproachable. As the evening drew on, we were gratified by noticing the wind shifting to the north, and a flush in the sky betokening frost.

"Egad, Will," said my uncle, rubbing his hands as we gained the portal of the Wisp, "if the weather hardens a bit, we'll have the cock in the mountain in a day or two."

That evening, as usual, we had a long gossip after dinner. My uncle had an inexhaustible budget of stories, most of them relative to an extinct race of wild Irishmen, whose doughty deeds on horse and foot, with gun and pistol, he well remembered. There was one anecdote which, as illustrative of Celtic pluck, I may be pardoned for repeating. I will tell it as nearly as possible in the manner that I heard it. My uncle used to call it

DICK POOLE'S JUMP.

Dick Poole's father came of a stock, the Pooles of Poolgarra, of hard drinkers and hard riders, who were never known to do a useful thing or an unkind act, and who were consequently very popular with the tenants. It need scarce be said that Poolgarra was in Ireland, and that the system of management pursued by the owners was such as to reduce the dimensions of the estate, until, when it came to the hero of this tale, there was little left of the ancestral acres. But Dick Poole cared naught for this. As long as he had the privilege of fishing and shooting over the old place (and the new-comers never refused him), and could procure enough of money from his agent to get drunk as often as he liked, he let the world wag, and saw the property slide from him with the equanimity of an impecunious philosopher. He had been weaned, so to speak, upon the bottle. When a boy, his worthy sire used to encourage him to sip stiff punch from a tumbler specially reduced in dimensions to suit his tender years. A gun was made for him with a similar view to the fitness of things. When he grew up, he was presented with a larger tumbler and a bigger gun. On one occasion he rode a steeplechase, and when he came in a winner, his father delightedly exclaimed, " Dick, I'm prouder of you at this moment *than if you wrote the Bible!*" His education was supposed to have been amply provided for when he could hold his own with the hounds and distinguish himself with a gun in the bogs or the stubble.

The consequence of this hereditary course of training was, that Dick became a dead shot, and possessed of a wonderful head for whisky. He disposed of farm after farm of his estate, until at length nothing was left him but the old house, which he stuck to, and an old retainer, Dan Doherty, who clung to his fortunes with a fidelity which might be described as melodramatic. Poole of course, from his habits, was not a welcome guest among the county families, though they universally admitted his right to consider himself of their caste. He kept up, however, a custom of visiting the officers who were stationed at a small garrison town in the neighbourhood; and it was at their mess, to which he was invited, that the circumstance arose, the sequel of which rendered his name a household word throughout the province.

During dinner, Poole conducted himself well enough. He was fortunately placed next a quiet sucking ensign; but when the claret was disposed of, when the major left the room, and strong waters were called on, Poole laid himself out, as was usual with him, for a hard night. A few of the men, seeing the rate at which he went, calculated on putting him under the table; but before Dick had shown the slightest token of undue exhilaration, several of his entertainers were talking thickly and laughing loudly. Hunting and shooting stories were exchanged with a crescendo of mendacity on the part of the narrators as the night advanced. Dick had set them all in a roar by describing how he had shot down every bird in a covey save one; "and I left him," shouted Dick, "to breed." At length the conversation turned upon swimming.

"Talk of swimming," put in Poole, "do you know the cliffs at the seaside of Poolgarra? I'll bet any man I'll jump off the highest part of those cliffs, and carry another fellow on my back."

A universal burst of laughter, and cries

of "Take you up, old boy! How much can you book for?" greeted this insane challenge.

When the noise had somewhat subsided, Lieutenant Browne, the senior lieutenant of the regiment, produced a betting-book, and said to Dick,—

"If you are serious, Mr. Poole, for a hundred you don't do it."

"Done!" replied Dick at once; and it was fixed there and then that the performance was to take place on the following Saturday.

For a wonder Poole walked off steadier than many of his hosts could on that night. Lieutenant Browne expressed himself well in to win; "for if the fool would be mad enough to attempt such a thing himself, there is no one living who would be idiot enough to go on his back," thought he. Next morning Poole told Dan Doherty how he had enjoyed himself at the barracks, and then quietly mentioned the bet, as if he made nothing of it. Dan for a few seconds could not speak a word for horror and surprise; at last he managed to stammer out,

"O Master Dick, Master Dick, what ever d'ye mane by it? Is it out av yer sinses ye are intirely?"

"No, you old goose, I'm not out of my senses," replied Poole. "I want to win a hundred pounds; and what's more, Dan," he went on coaxingly, "you must help me to win it."

"Begorra, thin, I won't!" burst out Dan with rebellious energy. "I've sarved you, man an' boy, this many a year; but hand or part or futt, so help me——"

"Look here, Dan. I don't intend to do it at all, and still I intend to gain the wager. We want it, as you know, badly."

"God help us, 'tis thrue for you, sir, we do," said Dan emphatically.

"Well, here's my plan. We'll be on the ground. You'll get on my back," (Dan made a forcible gesture of dissent,) "and just as we seem about to start, the police will be on the spot to stop us. _Thigun-thugh?_" (Do you take?)

"You mane that we're to put them up to it? Is that it, sir?"

"Yes, of course."

"But, thin, won't the bet be a dhraw, sir?"

"No, it won't. Do you think I'd make such a wager without taking care that I should have an advantage over these English boobies? Leave it to me, Dan. Follow my directions, and you'll find everything will be right. I'll go into the town myself to-day and speak to the head-constable."

The eventful morning arrived, a cold grey morning it was, in July. The officers were all on the ground looking over the cliff, which was fully from ninety to a hundred feet above the sea, and wondering whether Dick Poole would have the courage to carry out his wild enterprise. Dick exchanged greetings with them cordially, and brought forward Dan as his partner in adventure. That individual had already some misgivings touching the order of proceedings; and when Dick peremptorily ordered him to take off his clothes, he showed decided symptoms of his courage oozing, like that of Bob Acres, from his fingers' ends. Poole, however, whispered a few reassuring words in his ear. "Besides," reflected Dan, as his teeth chattered with the fright and cold, "I've tould the poliss meself, for fear iv any mistake. I wonder they're not here already."

Dan prolonged his unrobing as much as possible; but at length he stood trembling *in cuerpo*, and before he could distinctly realize the situation he found himself on his master's back. Glancing over his shoulder in mortal terror, he saw the glazed caps of the police approaching.

"Are they coming, Dan?" whispered Dick softly.

"Yis, master dear, yis; only hould on for a minit."

"Are they very near us, Dan?"

"Quite close, yer honour," responded Dan, now becoming easy in his mind.

At this moment a constable ran forward, breaking from the officers, who tried to intercept him. But what was Dan's terror, when Dick clutched him firmly by the legs, and then, with a shrill "Whaup!" like the war-shout of an Indian brave, gave a header literally into space over the cliff!

Dan says he found himself going down

under water almost as far as he had fallen from land. The place was several fathoms deep; and on their rising to the surface, Dick grabbed his comrade, and bore him safely to a boat which was lying under the precipice prepared for the event. So Dick Poole won the hundred pounds, and Dan Doherty was none the worse.

Sunday, of course, is a day of rest at the Wisp. My uncle is a rigid sabbatarian; to this extent at least, that neither his ox nor his ass, his man- nor his maid-servants, his pointers nor his setters, are exercised against their will on that occasion. The village of Arvine is about three miles from us, and Uncle Joe proposes that I should go with him there and see the peasantry hearing mass. As we walk or drive along the road we meet the congregation—the elder women in long hooded cloaks, the younger in shawls and caps, the men in quaint tailcoats and breeches—all bound in the same direction. Some of the strong farmers—well-to-do farmers—have outside cars, on either side of which the ladies of the family are hung as if in panniers, and on

which a fortunate swain is occasionally placed
on the board between the damsels, enjoying
the enviable perplexity of Captain Macheath.
There is generally quite a cavalcade of com-
moner vehicles or 'butts,' in which a bundle
of clean straw, or perhaps a feather-bed, forms
a soft and convenient flooring for the travellers,
and in these they bump along, merrily ex-
changing greetings with each other; and for
all of them Uncle Joe has a pleasant word,
which is as cheerfully and heartily reciprocated.
When we come to the edge of Glenaugh de-
cline, the sound of the winter torrent flows up,
and with it the ding-dong of the bell from the
chapel of Arvine, that lies in a cup-like valley
surrounded with rocks and trees.

As we near it the fall grows steeper, until it
is necessary to use great caution with a horse.
The view is more than pretty. We over-
take his reverence, Father O'Brien, on our
journey. The people respectfully salute him
as they pass on; but few go by without a
friendly personal smile from the good priest,
who for over thirty years has watched the
Christian flock of this remote parish. I leave my

uncle and Father O'Brien to pursue the path together, or to trot, should they ride, beside each other, and take a short cut of my own to the end of the hill.   Winding round the neck of Glenaugh roll the cars and the tumbril-like wagons, the road is dotted with black cloaks and red shawls, ding-dong clangs the bell still farther below me, while a squadron of crows wheel up in the sunshine, and then perch about amongst the tall firs, or amongst the branches of mountain-ash, in which the berries gleam as red as fire.   The brawling stream never ceases to talk hoarsely, as it were, in a multitude of voices, and if you listen keenly you can catch the thud and shout it makes as it leaps some thirty feet from a rock a quarter of a mile off.   But see! the people are pouring from the dell into the chapel.   Shall we join them?

If you please, we will not examine this humble house of prayer with critical eyes. There is, indeed, a pathetic interest in the mud floor, the white-washed walls, on which tears of damp flow down the faces of badly-painted saints; all this must be taken in connection with the intense devotion of three or four hundred poor creatures, to whom the solemn service read by the priest has an awful supernatural significance. This Celtic congregation at worship is a wholesome spectacle to witness, no matter what may be your religious creed. The dim aisle is crammed, the wide doors are thrown open, and the yard is covered with a kneeling multitude, to whom the voice of the priest floats out clearly and distinctly above the droning of the stream or the occasional sough of the wind through the trees around us. No soft and cushioned pews here; no hushing lullabies on a velvet-toned organ, by which the soul of a fat sinner may be comfortably rendered unconscious, while his snug carcass is, for the sake of respectability, paying its weekly compliment to the Almighty. Now all are standing up; the spell is broken; the gossips gather into groups; youngsters shyly pair off to walk home along a golden path, for even in Arvine and Glenaugh youth has its Arcadian period. Do you see the three strapping lads talking to a blind patriarchal man who stands upon the bridge? These three represent a committee, a deputation, what you will, waiting on Paddy Byrne, the dark (blind) piper, in order to arrange a meeting with him at the Arvine cross in the evening. I observe that besides the chapel there are two other buildings in the hollow. One is the national school and the teacher's dwelling ; the other belongs to the care-taker of Arvine wood. A very pretty woman comes to the schoolhouse-door, dressed in a rather extreme style of rustic Irish coquetry. She reminds me at once, for withal she has a matronly air, of the giddy wife of John Christie, whom you may remember in Scott's 'Fortunes of Nigel.' But there is no Lord Dalgarno to arouse the jealousy of a husband in this happy valley. One might stay here and dream one's existence away in peace.

Some demon of mischief inspires me to stroll down and ask the pretty schoolmistress—I have fixed on her quality by guesswork—for a light for a cigar. She smiles charmingly as she invites me inside to help myself to what I require. I speak of the weather, of Father O'Brien. She says, with a curtsey, that she knows me through my uncle, and asks me to take a seat. The room is tastefully though poorly furnished. Yes, she is (with a sigh) the wife of the national schoolmaster.

I detest being the recipient of confidences of people for whom I don't care a straw, and so I turn the conversation from the gude man to indifferent topics. As I rise to leave, I am confronted at the door by a big, raw-boned, ill-tempered-looking vagabond, who almost hustles me back into the centre of the apartment.

"I beg your pardon, sir," said the fellow sulkily; "I did't see you;" and at the same moment he stared at his wife with a suspicious evil look, for which I longed to give him a sound kicking. And so I conclude Arvine is not a paradise, at least for this ill-matched couple. Think of the woman tied for life within an acre of ground to a sulky jealous brute, and think of her decking herself with ribbons on the chance of being seen by some one, any one. Nor do I imagine the national scholars find their superior amiable or friendly. He seemed every inch a flogging Orbilius; and so, doubtless, in this apparently peaceful spot, one malignant wretch can make a very hell of passions in fifty little bosoms, and torture his toy wife to the full content of his sour temper. That schoolmaster as completely vulgarized Arvine in my mind as though I had seen a comic singer start out of the ground there, in the complete costume of a tomfool, yelling one of the idiotic staves by which he makes the income of an attorney-general.

My shooting experiences at the Wisp vary so little, that I do not care to weary you by recounting them. It is extraordinary, though, how I do not tire of eating game. I don't say I could stand *perdrix, toujours perdrix,* but I can assure you I have devoured *canard sauvage* with a monotonous persistence that ought to have a psychological result. As for hares—hares jugged, hares reduced to soup, hares in stews, hares roasted—I have partaken of leporine food to that degree, that I verily believe I should take to my heels at the sight of a greyhound. I shall have plenty of time, however, when my brief stay is over, to correct these consequences of a sportman's diet. But my chief luxury, I confess it, is a negative one. Who is it that says happiness consists in negations ? I never read a book, I never look at a newspaper; if one arrives, I give it to Jack Sullivan to use up instead of wads. He has already, through motives of economy, fired off a volume of Euclid and Valpy's Delectus over Murphy's bog. These works, he conceives, save him or his master the expense of purchasing a box of wads, my uncle giving them up for the purpose with a certain humorous alacrity. For the rest, I may tell you we are as little afraid of Fenians at the Wisp as we are of earthquakes or an attack of Iriquois. By cock and snipe (to use a picturesque oath), I should like to see them come near us ! Nor are we troubled with messages from ' Rory of the Hills ' or any other patriot of the same emphatic views. We burn our powder in a most peaceable fashion. I suspect Tim Callaghan of treason, but Tim cannot do much to effect the disintegration of the empire. Besides, your tailor has a natural tendency towards Radicalism, as Mr. Kingsley has typified in ' Alton Locke.' One story about Tim. In order to encourage native talent, I gave him instructions the other day to make

me a suit of clothes for country wear.   Tim's
notion of his art is to construct the gar-
ments with a steady view to tightness of ex-
pression, if I may use the phrase.   When I
got into his works, he exclaimed, in admiration
of the achievement he thought he had com-
passed, " Faix, yer honner looks as if you had
been *melted* into 'em."

CHAPTER III.

BEATING THE SPRINGS AND THE WOOD.

DEVOTED as Uncle Joe was to sport, and to
everything connected with it, he was well
versed in current literature, and had the most
motley stock of novels, out of which he de-
rived a peculiar kind of ironical diversion.
He had assigned a special department in his
library to the lady romancists, and he used to
say that all their productions pleased him,
from a particular point of view, equally.   In
bad weather we had generally a box of these
productions to open, which had been sent from

town by a literary acquaintance of ours, who occasionally spent a month in the winter with us, and who, in the way of business, was extensively furnished with what are called works of light reading. The novels we received appeared to have been operated on for some specific purpose, to judge by the manner in which certain passages were scored up, and leaves turned down; in fact, our London friend was a reviewer, and a popular performer in his line. We invited him over a few days ago, and the outside car has been despatched for him to the railway station about six miles off.

Mr. Staunton—Fred Staunton—was a quiet undemonstrative specimen of his order, who, considering his constant and indispensable attachment to the ink-pot, was as passionately interested in shooting or fishing as either my uncle or myself. We had to meet him the day he arrived Dr. Phelan, a practitioner who combined a knowledge of hunting and of medicine in equal proportions. The man neglected no opportunity of studying his profession or of understanding horses and how to ride to hounds. He never hesitated to give up a meet, however, to attend a poor patient; but his wealthier clients, and his connection extended through the entire county, could not rely upon him for either complimentary or unnecessary visits.

"Staunton, where would you like to go to-morrow?" asked my uncle, "I think we might try Doyle's Marshes."

"Wherever you like. I am afraid you will find I have fallen off in my shooting."

"Oh, come, don't try to be modest. A man no more forgets how to shoot, than he forgets how to swim or to skate, having once learned."

"I am sorry I can't join you, boys," says the Doctor, "but can't you drop in on me to dinner? You'll have to pass by the house, and you can send things for changing round in the morning."

This proposition was agreed to cheerfully.

I had a little difficulty in knocking up Fred in the raw morning, and duly pointed out his tub to him, at which he groaned, and begged for a respite until daylight at least. "Why, it is the middle of the night yet, Will, and we can't start in the dark."

" Discipline, sir, must be maintained at the 'Wisp.' No sluggards allowed on the premises. Your host has been up this hour, has seen to the dogs, ascertained the thickness of the ice in the tank (here Staunton shuddered, and snuggled himself further into his bedclothes), and has settled that we must alter our route, in consequence of the hard black frost."

When I retired, I heard a sigh of resignation, a sudden splash, and an involuntary yell and splutter from the room, and in twenty minutes, Staunton was with us in the breakfast parlour, looking rosy and fresh for a Londoner.

There is a bright turf fire in the parlour ; a pointer is lying on the rug before it, and appears to understand that Joe is about to consign him to his kennel again, for it would be simply cruelty to bring him into the field this weather. His companion, a thickly-furnished brown-coated retriever, will have his work cut out for him, and is taking pieces of hard biscuit sopped in milk from the hand of my uncle.

March is the word is the word now, march

for the soft fields, fields with springs in them, surrounded by screens of dwarf firs. It is as yet pitch dark. The road is as hard as steel, and the wind is absolutely numbing. Uncle Joe, Staunton and Jack Sullivan are smoking, but I always dread the effect of tobacco on my nerves immediately after breakfast.

Dawn comes, slowly and reluctantly at first, but when the sun once gets his shoulder up, the light steals on apace, and with it, hark! the pipe of the golden plover.

" Load, boys ! "

My uncle after this order, like a skilful general, points out the places we are to take, for you may be sure he knows the field in which the birds are.

Peeping cautiously over a hedge at a signal whistle from Joe, we see a big detachment of a stand in the centre of an orchard stubble.

My uncle surveys them ·with a view to measuring the distance. At that moment the sentinel bird once more gives a shrill warning, and in an instant the plover are on the wing, and rushing right into my face.

Bang ! bang ! hurrah ! they have been

turned, and are now exposed to a raking shot from my uncle, and then again are flurried into the corner in which Staunton lies in ambush.

Jack Sullivan cheers the first lucky exploit of the day, as he picks up nine dead, while Dick, the retriever, is chasing the cripples in a deliberate and knowing fashion.

Nothing puts a sportsman in better humour than to be successful in the start. " Hallo ! "

This exclamation is from my uncle, as he points to a distant field, from which a puff of gun-smoke is curling; his gesture is followed by a sharp hard report.

" Run down this moment, Jack, and see who that is. No one has leave here, except Doctor Phelan and Mr. Redmond.

Jack returns with word that it *is* Mr. Redmond, at which my uncle's features relax from a rather discontented expression to one of genuine welcome, which broadens and expands even more hospitably as we approach the gentleman referred to.

" Glad to meet you, Redmond ; why didn't you come up to the Wisp, or write ? Have you done anything ? "

"Well, Joe, I had scarce time as yet."

"What, not time to kill a hare? Now, Redmond, what has Bill Sliney there in the bag? Bill, you rascal, come here and show me."

"Begor, and 'tis a fine puss, sure enough," remarks Mr. Sliney, with a grin, as he pulls out of the capacious wallet slung on his shoulder, a hare of calf-like proportions.

Redmond and my uncle laughed heartily; the former was death on fur, and my uncle placed a jocose interdict on his shooting hares, which his friend treated with an indifference which served as a standing joke between them.

The sun was now bright, too bright indeed. The fields glistened and sparkled in the frost, and the mere exercise of walking was a delicious sensation.

We pass on to where a green patch of grass shows that the water is unfrozen about it. "Look out here for a snipe!" cries my uncle. "Staunton, you go forward, and try what you can do."

Fred steps in front, my uncle keeping a close watch on the little morass.

Up springs a snipe, and with him a teal! Staunton seems slightly flurried as he fires right barrel at the teal, left at the snipe. The teal drops like a stone, the snipe alters his swift, waggling flight to a sudden slow wave of the wings, his legs hang down, and then he turns straight round, and rises slowly over our heads to tumble as dead as his companion at our feet.

"You should take more time, Fred," remarks my uncle, who is never satisfied unless every bird shot at is killed, as he calls it, neat and clean.

Mr. Redmond is poking about for himself. We catch a glimpse of something brown darting between two bundles of withies, then *thud* from Mr. Redmond's gun, and Bill Sliney holds up in triumph another hare.

"Egad, Redmond, you'll have enough of hares to make a wig before the day is out," remarks my uncle, at which he and Mr. Redmond laugh consumedly, as they have been accustomed to do at the same venerable joke for twenty years at least.

When we arrive at the course of a swift brook, which the frost has been unable to

K

tame, according to a custom amongst us, my uncle is requested to take the first half-mile of it to himself, and give us a lesson in snipe shooting. Proudly, but with an initiatory apology, Joe moves a little aside from the bank, and then commenced 'a practice' that was only comparable to the performances of the billiard champion, when he gets in position for the spot stroke. In weather such as I have been describing, the snipe leave the frozen bogs and mountains, and pitch along the soft edges of the flowing streams. To see the cool deliberate deadly style in which my uncle, when six or seven would get up together, used to bring down his brace, was an instructive spectacle. No cripples, no fluttering, and hopping, and squeaking, followed after a shot from my uncle's gun. The bird was rid of his life before he could know it, and was frequently thumped so as to rebound from the earth by the charge of number eight at a distance—my uncle's invariable distance for snipe —of between twenty-five and thirty yards.

We were quite silent with admiration, and looked on without the least jealousy at the unrivalled veteran. At last, when he had made his seven brace without missing a single shot, or wounding a single bird, we gave him a cheer, led off by Jack Sullivan, who could no longer contain his enthusiasm, as he shouted, " The master for ever ! agin the whole of yiz," and he looked in with an interrogative and rather warlike air at Bill Sliney.

" Tom Walshe sometimes draws the ice off his ponds, Jack," said Joe to his assistant.

" Yes, sir, an' as he did last night, there mebbe a spot for the duck on 'em, yer honour."

" Just what I was thinking, Jack."

Tom Walshe's ponds are situate between the hollows of a heather-covered hill. It is requisite to walk very deftly and silently towards them.

My uncle calls a halt, and assigns to us our different routes of approach; no one is to put up his head to look at the pond until Joe whistles.

The manœuvres are executed with discretion, but result in nothing. The ponds are completely frozen, and there is no sign of a living thing near them.

" Well, better luck elsewhere, boys. Jack,

K 2

what do you think if we were to beat Inch Wood?"

"The cocks are in it, no doubt sir, an' I don't believe yer honour could do better."

There is a couple of miles of a walk to Inch Wood. The wood covers both sides of a glen through which a mountain torrent runs. It forms exactly a figure of this kind Road Hill Wood Wood River.

We send the beaters in amongst the trees and brushwood. Staunton and I take our places on the hill, my uncle and Tom Redmond guard the road. And now the cheery cry of "Hie cock! Hie cock!" resounds amongst the timber, together with the cracking of the cudgels against the branches and ferns, and the hollow roar and boom of the stream in the valley. "Hie cock! Hie cock!" shouts Jack Sullivan. "Hie cock! Hie cock!" yells his assistant bushwhacker. "*Mark cock!*" yells Jack, and we look eagerly, with our guns ready, along the top line of trees.

There is a dead silence for a second which is broken by the report of a gun, and then a shout from my uncle proclaims that an addition has been made to the bag.

A hedge runs through the field in which we are walking. I am helping Staunton over it, having gained the top and laid down my gun.

"*Mark cock! Mark cock!*"

Two splendid birds rush from the wood within ten yards of us. I let go Staunton's hand, and he flops into a thicket of briars. I make a hopeless, staggering shot, and tumble back on him myself. I am sorry to say that Dick, the retriever, was never so near coming to an untimely end, as he was at that moment. The charges from both barrels struck the ground about ten yards from where I fired, within a few inches of his ear. Serve him right for neglecting his manners, and going over a hedge without express orders, before a gun.

Staunton cuts rather a rueful figure as he extricates himself from the prickly furze.

"Mark cock!"

"Ha! he has it."

"Mark cock! Mark cock!"

Bang, Bang, Bang, Bang! from my uncle's side.

"What's that, Jack?"

"The masther, sir, has shot a couple o' birds that time, and Mister Redmond killed a rabbit wud both barrels."

And so on, until we arrive at the bridge at the end of the wood, where we find the luncheon hamper waiting for us, and after levying a toll on its contents, we consult my uncle as to our campaign.

"You must come on to the Doctor's with us, of course, Tom?"

"Yes, he expects me, I believe, and whether he did or not, I should go."

"Then we have only an hour and a half to shoot at most, and the sooner we start off again the better. Mr. Staunton, there is no use in your shirking your work."

Fred is not in as good a condition as the rest of the party, and rather reluctantly allows himself to slide from the parapet of the bridge on which he has been sitting.

We shot with a steady success on our route to Draycourt, Dr. Phelan's residence. Draycourt was an exceedingly pretty spot. Even now, in the depth of winter, though the old avenue trees were bare, there was a solemn venerable, warm look about the old red brick house, on whose panes the flush of the sinking sun was glowing. Draycourt was haunted by vast congregations of starlings, who at evenfall, arrived in immense flocks from all parts of the surrounding country, and retired for the night into the recesses of an evergreen copse, which fringed the two sides of the lawn. When we arrive at the gate, we were met by the worthy Doctor himself, who insisted at once on knowing how we had got on.

"You will find everything in your rooms," he said, "and be ready for the dinner-bell in half-an-hour."

It adds much to the enjoyment of a day's shooting, to know that you will at the end of it meet with pleasant cheery faces, instead of retiring into the dismal solitude of an inn, where the cooking is vile, and the accommodation generally insufficient. My uncle's modest establishment was perfect of its kind, but the Doctor had the advantage over us of putting a lady at his table, and a very charming lady too. Mrs. Phelan could enter quickly into our talk on sporting subjects, and could show an intelligent concern when our disasters and successes were recorded. Tom Redmond was capital company, and therefore his conversation could not be written down for a book; no really bright, unforced chat bears decanting into print. When dinner was over, we went at once into the drawing-room for coffee, and after a couple of hours' music, Uncle Joe called time, but the doctor insisted upon putting us up for the night. To this arrangement we acceded. Staunton and I exchanged telegraphic nods and signals as we passed up stairs, and in accordance with them, I joined him for a cigar.

"Did I ever tell you how I came across my wife, in Ireland?" said Fred.

"No, I heard you married an Irish lady."

"Well, the story is worth telling, if you are not too sleepy to listen to a yarn."

"I should be delighted to hear it. Give the fire a poke, and go ahead."

Staunton took a few very vigorous puffs, and throwing himself into a roomy arm chair, told his tale as closely after the following fashion as I can remember :—

THE EDITOR'S STORY.

"Wanted an experienced editor of Liberal views to conduct a journal in the provinces."

Such was the announcement that struck my eye as I glanced on the front page of a literary journal. I wanted an excuse for leaving London, and thought this post would just suit me. I had a small income independent of a remunerative connection with reviews and periodicals, and if the situation should turn out to be a poor one in a monetary way, I could afford to put up with it for a short time. I called on the agent to whom the advertisement referred.

"Well, sir," he replied to my preliminary questions, "I doubt if the place will suit you; the salary offered is very small."

"I don't so much care for that at present. Where should I have to go to, and what is the name of the paper?"

"Here is a copy of it."

"Why, this is in Ireland!"

"Yes, sir; we have had many gentlemen

calling here; who inquired no further when they ascertained that fact."

" But how is it the proprietors are willing to employ an Englishman, as I presume they are from your agency in the matter?"

" I can scarce tell, sir. My correspondent on the subject is a lady, who writes as if she were the owner of the journal, and perhaps she is."

The ' Castletown Eagle'—the name rather tickled my fancy, and I had no objection to go to Ireland. It would serve my purpose as well as any other quarter of the globe. The man seemed astonished at the alacrity with which I closed with the miserable terms on which the desk of the '.Eagle' was offered.

"You can write," I said, as I was leaving, "to say you have secured an editor, and a cheap one. With reference to qualification, you can say whatever you like; but, on second thoughts, perhaps you had better simply state that you believe I am capable of doing the work."

"Very good, sir. I shall let you know when they are ready for you."

A week after this I had taken my seat in the ' Wild Irishman' train, from Euston ter-

minus, bound for the extreme south of the
county of Cork. As I leaned back in the
carriage, I felt a certain boyish delight at my
escape from the London round of life, which
was becoming more or less wearisome to me.
On arriving at Holyhead I noticed three ladies
on the platform, who seemed in a distracted state
with their luggage. There was no gentleman
with them apparently, and the porter was listen-
ing in a surly and uninterested manner to their
nervous description of a missing box. I went
forward, and inquired if I could be of any
assistance. They thanked me, and explained
that they had put the box into the carriage
with them—where it was ultimately found,
shoved far back under a seat, when the surly
porter condescended to search for it. One of
the ladies, while directing the man, had given
me a shawl and cloak to hold, and when the
little incident was over, I found myself follow-
ing the party on board the steamer. They
went down to the cabin, but I remained on
deck, and was about to hand over my charges
to the stewardess, when the owner of the shawl
reappeared.

"Thank you," she said smiling, as I offered to help her on with the cloak and to wrap her in the shawl; "I could not remain below, the morning is so fine."

"I think we are pretty sure of a calm passage."

"I am glad of that for my companions' sake. I am a good sailor myself."

"Are you not afraid of the chill? there is always a cold mist over the sea at this hour."

"O, not the least afraid."

I remember with a clear distinctness how our conversation grew, but I doubt whether it would be as interesting to others as it was to me. In fact, before the sun rose—and a beautiful dawn it was, flushing over the far edge of the green waves—we had become strangely confidential. Perhaps I ought rather to say *I* had. The lady listened with interest enough to encourage me, and at last I told her what was bringing me to Ireland.

"I am to edit a paper for an old woman."

"Indeed! it was a strange notion of yours, this adventure. How odd it would turn out if she were a widow and you were to marry her ! There is a subject for three volumes for you at once."

" I should be sorry to marry in Ireland. Irish ladies, I understand——"

A little nod of the head, half satirical and half coquettish, warned me off the blunder I was about to make.

" But I didn't think you were Irish."

" Yes, quite Irish; and very proud of the fact, I assure you."

I hastened at once to apologize for the tone in which I had spoken. She took my explanation in the best good-humour.

The bay of Dublin was now opening before us, and I can at this moment call to mind the loveliness of that summer morning : the deep emerald tinge of the sea, the Wicklow hills, like purple clouds in the distance, the heavy-eyed gulls floating curiously across, and sometimes getting tangled in the smoke and seeming to dissolve in it to the size of white butterflies. There were as yet very few people on deck ; but the quay draws nigh, and one by one the passengers appear.

" I think I had better say good-bye to you

now." And she held out her hand to me with a sweet unconscious frankness.

"Good-bye! I trust we may come across each other again. Perhaps you would tell me your name?"

She smiled for a second, and then, with an expression full of fun, glanced from me to one of her boxes lying outside the great deck pyramid of luggage.

I understood her at once. We parted, and I carefully wrote down "Miss Wentworth, Mountjoy Square, Dublin," the name and address inscribed on the trunk.

Late the next night I arrived at the Castletown Arms, having performed the last twenty miles of the journey on a stage coach. My first impressions of Castletown were similar to those to which Johnson gave such emphatic utterance when Boswell told him " Sir, we are now in Scotland!" In the morning I found it impossible to procure a cold bath; but, instructed by a garrulous waiter, I found my way to a river which promised capital angling. On returning from a plunge and a swim, I went into a shop to purchase a copy of the 'Castletown Eagle,' and I thought I could scarce do better than have a chat with the shopkeeper touching its local circulation and influence.

" Have I an *Aigle*, is it ? Be gor I have, bad luck to them for *Aigles*."

" I thought it was considered a very good paper."

" Ye don't know what they call it in Cark, thin ? " replied the fellow, with that sort of indescribable grin which comes over an Irishman's face when he is enjoying the foretaste of a joke ; " they calls the *Aigle* the *Goose*, and in my opinion they're right."

Notwithstanding my very limited association up to that period with the journal in question, I confess it was with no slight feeling of annoyance that I walked to breakfast after this account of it.   While at the repast, I remembered that the first thing I had to do was to see the gentleman whom I was to succeed, and who I had stipulated was to remain in office at least a fortnight after my arrival.

" James, take in my cawrd," I heard a deep voice growl from the hall outside the coffeeroom ; and the waiter appeared, and handed me a piece of pasteboard on which was engraved, "Mr. Joseph O'Brien, 'Castletown Eagle.'"

I rose to meet Mr. O'Brien, who was indeed the retiring editor of the 'Eagle;' and as the door opened, a very tall powerfully-built man, rather coarse and florid-looking, but with handsome features, dressed in sporting costume, and with a brace of red setters at his heel, stood before me.

"How d'ye do, sir? I'm glad to see you," said Mr. O'Brien heartily, and with an honest ring in his voice that took my fancy at once ("To hale, ye divils!"—this to the setters, who were sniffing curiously now at my legs). "I hope you had a pleasant voyage."

I told him I had, and asked him to join me at breakfast, which he did; and when it was over he began immediately, at my request, to give me a notion of the duties I was about to enter on. The 'Eagle,' I learned, was the sole property of a Mrs. Brady, whose husband had started and conducted it many years before. The editorial functions to be discharged consisted in writing two leaders (I am afraid Mr.

O'Brien called them "laders,") in the week, and in controlling the movements of a solitary reporter, who "did" the petty sessions, meetings of boards of guardians, and such musical and dramatic criticism as arose out of the occasional visit of a travelling theatrical company, or a concert of Castletown amateurs.

"Mrs. Brady is mighty stiff and stuck up; ye'll see but little of her. We've both to dine there to-day, though, and you can judge for yourself."

The opinion I formed of Mr. O'Brien was that he was a clever idle fellow; and I could perceive that he was not in the least annoyed at having to surrender his post to me.

Mrs. Brady resided outside the town, which contained, I should think, about ten thousand people, and was a prosperous place enough, as such towns went. Her house was prettily situated, with a short lawn running down to the river. As we were walking up to the house, Mr. O'Brien (who wore a string of artificial flies round his hat) told me he had landed many a three and four pound trout on the grass quite close to us.

L

Mrs. Brady was picking some flowers which were trained round a little pillar near the steps, and she turned round to greet us.

"You have had a long distance to come, Mr. Staunton. I trust we can make your stay with us agreeable."

Mrs. Brady spoke without a trace of the brogue. The dinner passed off pleasantly enough, and I found I could get on very well indeed with Mrs. Brady. During the course of the repast Mr. O'Brien intimated that a boy was to bring him letters from the office in the evening, and "my rod too," the ex-editor continued.——"I thought you wouldn't mind me making a few casts in the garden ;" this half-apologetically to Mrs. Brady.

"Not at all," answered our hostess graciously; "and I trust you will be fortunate."

In due course the boy came, with a rod and landing-net, and Mr. O'Brien disappeared.

"I wanted to have a chat with you, Mr. Staunton, said Mrs. Brady.

We walked together into the garden, and I learned all about the politics and supporters of the 'Eagle.' I ventured to ask why Mr. O'Brien was to be deposed.

"I think I may tell you, Mr. Staunton, although the reason is rather of a private nature. I didn't want him to make love to my daughter."

"Your daughter?"

"Yes. She is at present on a visit to a relative of hers in Dublin. In fact, it was at her request I am obliged to remove our editor, with whom, in a business way, I have no particular fault to find. He was constantly addressing verses to Margaret in his 'Poet's Corner.' When he became acquainted with my reasons, he took matters very quietly, and so good-humouredly, that we remain, as you perceive, on the friendliest terms."

"Then he does not depend for his income altogether on the 'Eagle'?"

"No; he has a small farm a few miles from here, and I think is rather glad than otherwise at being released from a fixed occupation. But, Mr. Staunton, there is something I want to say to you, if I may."

"Certainly."

L 2

"Well, to tell you the truth, I dread in your case a similar difficulty."

I confess I felt considerably vexed. What business had the old woman to suppose that I was going to fall in love with her daughter? Most likely an Irish country girl, with a milk-maid complexion, and a few boarding-school graces.

"I can assure you, Mrs. Brady, that there is no danger of anything of the kind occurring; I am not a marrying man."

"I only wished to have your word on the subject; it would render our intercourse here less constrained, and I expect Margaret home in three weeks."

The conversation then turned off from this topic; but I could not prevent myself from feeling very angry, and registering a silent vow that I would show both Mrs. Brady and her daughter that I had no desire for the honour of an alliance with the family.

Nothing could equal Mr. O'Brien's courtesy and attention to me when I got the 'Eagle' into hand. Our politics were rather parochial than European, but there were occasions in

which we considered it essential to warn Prussia,
or threaten France, or refer to our difficulties
with Central Asia. Our parliamentary repre-
sentative, who had promised to develop the
mining resources of Castletown, had to be
looked after; so had Mr. Disraeli and a town
commissioner, who was a tailor in private life,
and who addressed letters to me signed an
' Ouvrier.' By the time I understood my busi-
ness I was thoroughly disgusted with it, and yet
it certainly amused me. I shall never forget a
scene at a public dinner in the town-hall the
first week of my arrival. The banquet was
given in connection with an agricultural society,
which had been started by a new English pro-
prietor. Mr. O'Brien sat next to me during
the banquet, which was of the most substantial
description. He seemed most anxious that the
dignity of the press should be duly asserted,
although his mode of expressing his sentiments
on the matter did not appear to me to be of the
most impressive kind. For instance—as it
happened more than once—if we required any-
thing, Mr. O'Brien announced his wants in
this fashion : " Waiter, a fork for the press !

Potatoes for the press, waiter! Waiter, salt for the press!" and so on.

There was a stout farmer opposite me, whose performances on the beef and mutton were simply wonderful. This gentleman appeared, however, infinitely perplexed and disturbed by the tunes of a German band, which was hired to play in the progress of the festival. If he had an ear for music I don't wonder at it, for I seldom heard anything more discordant; but I think his dislike arose from a less fanciful cause. He was, at the eighth repetition of a waltz, driven beyond endurance, and roared out 'Stop!' in so commanding a tone, that every one looked round. There was a dead silence for a moment, and the hideous orchestra was struck dumb; a shout of laughter from the company, however, sent it on again in full swing. Some ladies came in to look at us, and hear the speeches; when I took a note of their dowdinesses, I was more than ever tickled at the idea of being warned against the fascinations of a Castletown belle.

It was a fortnight after this (the winter was fast coming on and the river was loaded with brown leaves) that I spent an evening with Mrs. Brady ; and, on the arrival of the post, she told me her daughter was returning the next day. "I have a bad cold, and perhaps you would meet Margaret at the post-office for me," she said. Of course I assented, and accordingly found myself in due time waiting outside the inn at which the ramshackle 'Lightning' was expected. I was a little early, and spent the spare minutes smoking and speculating with some interest on the kind of girl she might be with whom I was not to fall in love on any account. In a quarter of an hour I heard the old-fashioned guard's horn, and a minute afterwards I was opening the door for a young lady whose face and head were so enveloped in a warm cloak that I could not distinguish her features. I simply introduced myself by saying, "Miss Brady?" and, receiving a nod in reply, I handed my charge out, and then got her boxes off the roof. When this was done I turned round, and saw standing next to me my fair companion of the Holyhead steamboat. She was laughing heartily, and putting out her hand said,

"I hope the 'old woman' and you are getting on well, Mr. Staunton. You see I have waited all this while to surprise you."

I scarce knew what to say. The explanation of the mystery was simple enough. Instead of pointing to one of her own boxes to direct me to an address, she had shown me a trunk which did not belong to her at all.

"And then you know, when you told me what you were going to do, I knew all about it, and wanted to have some fun with you when I came home."

Upon reaching the house, I was still confused, and felt an odd feeling of regret and pleasure. Mrs. Brady kissed her daughter affectionately, and I took my leave. I passed over the little bridge leading into the town on the way to my lodgings. Without being much of a poet or a mooner, I have a constant hankering after scenery. I could not help lingering on the bridge of planks to look at the shining stream passing off into the dark under a curve of low hills, and I began to regret my promise to Mrs. Brady.

Mrs. Brady was good enough to express the

greatest satisfaction with my management of her 'Eagle'; and, in truth, that bird was soaring high in the estimation of the subscribers, who had begun to increase in numbers. I had gone into whatever society there was in the place, but had dropped it on the shortest trial. I still kept Mr. O'Brien with me. I did so, because, as I did not seriously contemplate living for any length of time in Castletown, it would be as well that Mr. O'Brien should be prepared to take up the running, as, as far as I could see, time had removed the objection which Mrs. Brady had to him. I was heartily fond of snipe-shooting, and, with O'Brien's aid and companionship, I managed to pass—

There is no use in beating about the bush in this manner; I fell ignominiously over head and ears in love with Margaret Brady. I have a suspicion that O'Brien knew my secret, and felt a grim satisfaction at my sufferings. I think he was waiting with a prophetic grin for the time when I should also break out in the 'Poet's Corner' of the 'Eagle.' But I remembered my resolution and pledge, and the rather insidious way in which it was drawn from me. Meanwhile Margaret and I became the best of friends. I was accustomed, when the paper was out, to spend the next day on the moors, and in the evening went to Mrs. Brady, who always expressed herself happy to see me. Margaret played charmingly. It was pleasant in the turf-glow to listen to the weird and intricate skeins of notes lit with poetry, like some one's brown hair with threads of gold. I sat as far away from the piano as I could; at least I generally did, except once, and then I couldn't help it. I sat in a chair by my darling's side, and, as she bowed her head over the notes, my face was very close to hers. There was only one thought in our minds, and we both knew it. With an impulse I could no more help than I could help breathing, I touched her lips with mine. It was only for one instant. On went the ripple of the waltz as though nothing had happened; on it went, but the notes were freighted now, not with the mere fancies of the artist, but with the burden of our own hopes for the future. When the waltz was over,

Margaret went from the room.   I did not see her again that evening, and I had to wake Mrs. Brady to wish her good-night.

Next morning I called on Mrs. Brady.   I was resolved, at least, to tell as straightforward a story as I could, and if she determined to keep me to my word, why, at the worst I should have to do so.   She looked very grave when I met her.   She heard me out with a cold politeness, and then asked me how soon I could complete my arrangements for leaving Castletown.   There was a hard, cold, inexorable tone in her voice, and a contempt in it that stung me to the quick.   I was ready to leave at once, but——

"You have broken your promise, Mr. Staunton ; I permitted your visits here, trusting to it.   The sooner we part the better.   I think I can manage to reconcile my daughter to the loss she will sustain by your departure."

"Can I see her before I leave ?"

"Certainly not."   And the old lady opened the library door with a gesture that, taken with her white set face, was not encouraging to me.

I went down to the office of the 'Eagle,' and without hesitation related the circumstances to Mr. O'Brien.

"Bedad, it's an ugly business," said that gentleman. "Does Margaret like you?"

"She does," I answered, and was almost sorry for speaking so abruptly, the good fellow's face showed so much genuine sadness.

"Well, she's a sweet girl," he remarked after a pause. "Look here, when are you to leave?"

"To-morrow, if you will resume your old post."

"I'll do anything for you, my boy," said this thoroughly loyal-hearted Irishman, "anything for you—and Miss Margaret," he added with a slight effort; "but I see nothing for it, except for you to run away with her."

"That won't do. I deceived her mother already; I'll not take her daughter from her in a sneaking fashion now."

"Then let me think over it. I can always consider best with the gun under my arm; and I'm going out for a crack at the plover now. In the evening I'll tell you my plans."

I spent the day packing up; and when that

task was over, I walked through the little room, and down to my favourite lounge on the bridge, from which I could catch a glimpse of Mrs. Brady's house. How sick and miserable I felt!

I returned, and wrote a letter to Margaret. I did not know whether it would be delivered to her or not; but it was a relief to me to write it. Just as Mr. O'Brien made his appearance with a well-filled bag, I had in reply a short note from Margaret. She was as miserable as I was. I would not forget her, would I? And she would so like to see me once more, if possible, before I went. If Mr. O'Brien spoke to mamma something might be done. I handed the note to O'Brien. He read it without a word.

"It is rather cruel of Miss Margaret to make me an ambassador in this cause," he said; "but I'll stand to you."

And off he started for Mrs. Brady's house at once.

I walked down to the bridge again. I watched the river with a half-vacant, half-stupid stare. I suddenly felt some one next to me. It was Margaret.

"I would see you—before you—before you —you—"

"Dearest, I will write to you constantly, and I hope to have a home to offer you shortly. If your mother persists—"

"Why did you make such a silly promise to her?"

This was said with an air of melancholy coquettishness.

"Because I didn't know who you were."

We almost forgot for a while that we were to part. I walked with her to the gate of the house. Margaret turned pale when we came in view of the modest mansion; and I was trembling all over. We halted on the steps of the entrance-porch. We could not, I believe, to save our lives have spoken a word at the moment. Both Margaret's hands were in mine; and they seemed to cling and to linger there, as if they would never leave their resting-place.

"Mrs. Brady's compliments, and will ye both come in?" calls aloud Mr. O'Brien from the garden.

The sentence was like the reading of a reprieve to a condemned criminal. We understood at once that Mr. O'Brien had been successful in his mission; and Margaret turned round and gave him a hearty kiss.

"I pitched into your mother, Miss Margaret," said the noble creature. "I told her the 'Aigle' might go to the divil if she acted harshly to you."

And so we went into tea; and Mrs. Brady saluted me on the cheek, and silently ratified the negotiation that had been so fortunately conducted by Mr. O'Brien.

In a month Margaret and I once more travelled together in a steamer, and took up our residence in town. The 'Eagle' now flourishes under the able editorship of our friend. I have never, as you may suspect, regretted my short connection with that influential journal; and I take a peculiar interest in still reading it; for Mr. O'Brien sends it to us regularly. Mrs. Brady has been entirely reconciled to me for my breach of promise, and occasionally condescends to visit us, without remaining longer than a well-regulated mother-in-law should.

"You must be tired, Will; good-night!" said Staunton, as he finished his story.

"Not at all. Do stay and have another weed."

"No; remember we must be up and doing in the morning. Your uncle has already cut out our work for us."

Next day there was a thaw, the whole landscape was dripping, but luckily there was no rain. Tom Redmond went off home, but Staunton, Uncle Joe, and I shot our way back to the 'Wisp.' The snipe lay capitally, and my uncle's performance was again of surpassing artistic excellence.

Three weeks fled on in this fashion, and at length Staunton and I took our departure together from the 'Wisp.' I never saw my uncle again. He died suddenly, and when I was too far off even to be in time to be present at his funeral. He sleeps in an old country graveyard, overshadowed by the hills, girt by the moors, and above which the wild cry of the plover and the clang of winter-sailing geese are heard. The 'Wisp' is deserted and broken up. I am sole heir of the eccentric library, and of the rods and guns that ornamented so appropriately our little cosy nook. These relics are full of touching memories to me, as most things are which belong to us before we have grown silly enough to be a little wise and a little selfish.

NOTES ON SHOOTING.

CHAPTER I.

COCK SHOOTING.

THIS sport has been compared in excitement to the chase properly so called; to flush and knock over a woodcock being thought by many who are experienced alike in hound, horse, and gun, to be as pleasant a feat as to ride across country and come in well at the death. One advantage, at least, cock shooting possesses——it is no mere tame holiday sport. You do not bring your woodcocks up by hand as you may your pheasant, you cannot flank them like partridges, nor need you pay heavy rents to get at them as you do for grouse. Then to follow this game is not so distressing as to follow snipe, and——what to some people is always a consideration of some importance —the birds are larger. Again, cock shooting tries a man's hand with every variety of shot. It is out of the question to determine, when a dog points, or when the cheery sound of " Mark cock !" rings through the wood, whether the snap or the mode deliberate must be adopted as the most suited for adding to the contents of the bag. Naturalists tell us that the eyes of the cock are made for feeding in the twilight or in the dusk, that it is a nocturnal fowl, as liable to blunder in the daytime as Minerva's pet when startled from an ivy bush into the noontide sun. This we shall not dispute ; but it is a fact that a cock when flushed in a grove of thick firs will often dart swift as a swallow through the trees, twirling in and out between them, and often when the gun is levelled give a sudden toss and tumble over the branches into the sky line, where he sometimes leaves his soul or his instinct: being caught upon the very hop, as it were, by a gentleman duly posted and otherwise qualified to interrupt the manœuvre. Many theories are adduced to account for this phenomenon,

M 2

amongst them that the cock's long bill is as
sensitive as the whiskers of the cat, and that he
feels his way with it; any one, however, who
has seen the performance we refer to would not
suspect that it was done after that method.

The woodcock begins to arrive in this coun-
try as early as September, but in very small
numbers.   In October large flights come over,
but in November the main contingents put in
an appearance.   When they first land they
drop into all sorts of odd places.   As our sea-
coasts are generally sparsely furnished with
heavy coverts, the cocks seek shelter in hedge-
rows, in patches of furze or gorse; but they
are especially fond of secreting themselves in
or about holly bushes.   We recommend any
of our readers who may be on the look-out
for them near the shores in the early part of
the season, never to neglect beating well
hedges of holly or even isolated clumps of
that tree.   They are easy shots when flushed,
when they first come in.   Some of the sport-
ing papers have spoken of them as being as
" plump and fat as butter " after their ocean
voyage.   As far as my own experience goes,

cocks shot near the shore (at the time of their arrival) are invariably thin and feeble; and, in fact, so weak are they that in some parts of Ireland they are watched and preyed upon by hawks that would never tackle with such a quarry if the birds had been in condition. They revive wonderfully in a short time, and for the reason that they are closer to their feeding though not to their hiding-grounds than when they seek the drier regions of wood and heather. The cock feeds upon the worms found in swamps and marshes, and this fare is abundant in the fens; but being of all things a shy secretive bird, it leaves even good diet for the sake of security.

There are many ways and places in which to seek for cock. The bird is shy of artificial coverts, however naturally made. The cock seems to suspect the snug haunts established for the pheasant. The best shooting is generally to be had in larger woods or fir groves, especially if these are in the neighbourhood of a wet meadow or a bog. In the recesses of the wood the bird lies all day, whether asleep or awake we believe nobody has yet discovered,

although it is supposed that at this time the
bird has his siesta. Here a number of beaters
are absolutely necessary ; and you may either
choose or have a walk chosen for you, or wait
at the skirts of the thicket or wood. Should
the ground be covered with brown fern and
dry grass, so much the better for the chances
of a find. If you are within the enclosure you
have no child's play to make good shooting.
The light is not unseldom defective, and when
a beater shouts ' Mark cock !' it requires a quick
eye to detect the side the bird has taken while
it is within range. Snap shots are almost in-
variably the best on such occasions, and it is
requisite to aim considerably in advance of the
cock, often perhaps with a couple of trees'
difference between the spot in which you catch
a glimpse of him and the spot at which you
fire. To effect this with decent success re-
quires more skill with a fowling-piece than any
other sport with a gun that we know of. It is
far better, however, if you have the selection,
to choose an outside post—if possible on a high
ground which overlooks the wood. Favourite
resorts of cock are valleys, narrow passes with

steep woods at either side, and a stream with a margin of soft ready soil running between. Stand on the alert outside the quarter of the slope that is being searched, and when the monotonous whish and whack of the beater's stick is diversified by a sudden shout of ' Mark cock !' even though you hear the shot fired from within, keep a sharp look-out, as, if the bird is missed, he is as likely as not, after darting some fifty yards through the cover, to rise above it, and then your time comes. Besides, it frequently happens that the beaters send out numbers of birds they never mark or see. It is a dangerous practice to beat two sides of a gully, such as we refer to, simultaneously. It is almost impossible in such a case to avoid accidents. The heights across which some one is sure to fire are on a level, and the only persons safe are the beaters, who enjoy for once comparative immunity. If a bird rises from the wood without being shot at from inside, and appears to be beyond range, it is as well to stoop down so as to hide from him. He may then pitch within sight. Now this is a fact which is again difficult to reconcile with the notion that a cock is as blind as an owl in the daylight. Clumber spaniels, low-sized dogs that can run busily, are the best for this sort of shooting. We should also recommend the outsider, whom we have been advising, to furnish himself with a good retriever. When a bird falls over the trees it is not easy to find him, and occasionally he cannot be found at all, being stuck, perhaps, wings outstretched in the upper branches. When the ground has been thoroughly searched for a dead bird, and you are pretty sure as to the spot, it is a good plan to shake the trees in the vicinity. After beating thick coverts, if there is a well-clothed heather moor in the neighbourhood, there the sport should be followed up. The moor should be closely beaten, and on this occasion the setters and the pointers may be used. The birds not being long in the place, the scent is often not powerful enough to draw the dogs, and so they should be treated with indulgence for faults of nose; besides the cock runs very fast and in a zigzag fashion, as if he quite understood the intentions of the sportsmen. On some moors broad reaches of withered fern and stone, interspersed with shallow pools, are to be found. These quarters should be cautiously approached, especially after the coverts have been emptied. Cocks often make for them, and when they do will fly wildly, never allowing a dog near them. A cock springing from the heather or the ferns gives much the same sort of a shot as the snipe, but you must be prepared for surprises, of which the snipe seems to know nothing. Now and again, as a bowler in desperate shift tries a slow sneaking ball what time the batsman is expecting a cracker, the woodcock, when you think he is about to bound off, hangs heavily on his wings for a baffling instant, and so lets your hasty cartridges pass right over his queer triangular head.

The conditions of shooting and pursuing all game birds are subject to change according to the weather. In frost and snow, especially, the rules for seeking game must be entirely revised. During severe weather, snow especially, the cock will be mostly discovered in the same description of quarters frequented by his cousin the snipe under similar circumstances, with this

difference, however.   The cock must have
bushes to hide in.   A splendid day's sport may
be had by a man who is independent enough
to take the field alone during the white, crisp,
snowy weather, when the air is as reviving as a
draught of champagne. As the woodcock seems
averse after his one great feat of locomotion to
repeated displays of the same kind, even under
stress of weather, he prefers to seek for his
livelihood as close to his familiar haunts as he
can.   A glen in which the sun is shining, and
through which a gurgling stream, yet unbound
by the frost, struggles through tangled branches
of thorn interspersed with holly ; a hedge
crusted with warm moss and overhung with
dwarf trees ; patches of gorse from which the
snow has thawed in half-reclaimed lowlands—
such are a few of the localities into which the
cock goes when the thermometer is at freezing
point.   And at such times it is necessary to
beat very closely indeed, so that we must
qualify the assertion about the pleasures of
complete solitariness during the ramble ; a boy
with a stick is all that will be required, and
wherever he cannot go tell him to pitch a

stone, and have your finger on the trigger the moment it drops. In such weather a pointer, setter, or even a Clumber is not of service, but a retriever will be useful. When a cock is wounded it will hide itself with great ingenuity, seeking nooks and corners which, from the hue of the ground, the old grass, fallen leaves, or withered brambles, are exactly *en suite* with its own russet garb.

It is a pity that in the northern parts of Europe, where these birds breed, their eggs are considered a greater luxury than even the eggs of the plover amongst us, and should fetch a high price. The consequence is, of course, a great diminution in the numbers that come over to us. Formerly it was believed that the flight of cocks was made by the moon, that they required moonshine, and travelled by and put off their journey until the almanac was propitious. The theory is now almost as obsolete as the belief that the barnacle mussel is the father and mother in one of the barnacle goose. The ill wind from the north and the north-east that blew of late must have brought us good in the shape of numerous woodcocks,

for the wind really seems to influence the start-
ing of our welcome guests. Very few of the
birds breed in this country, and, indeed, there
is not much encouragement for them to do so,
as, whenever a nest is discovered by a game-
keeper it is brought at once to his master as a
curiosity. We often hear complaints of the
disappearance of certain fauna before our
triumphs in drainage and railways, but the fact
is that we offer a sort of premium for the de-
struction of everything of the kind unusual,
by giving notoriety to the stupid oaf who stalks
the last bittern or robs the nest of the over-
courageous woodcock. In France thousands
of woodcocks are caught in nets hung upon
trees, and this sort of poaching is pursued
occasionally in England on a much smaller
scale, by placing nets on the edges of woods on
the line of flight taken by the birds on their
way to the feeding grounds in the evening.
Ireland is, perhaps, *par excellence*, the country
for cock shooting, and this year, we learn, the
birds have been passing over in unusual num-
bers. We hear the same report of England
and Wales, so that the prospects of the season

for the sport are altogether above the average. There is one thing we may be sure of, however, that no matter how many thousands or tens of thousands of woodcocks may be netted or shot in France or in Great Britain, we shall have to pay famine prices for them in our homes. Prices of game seem altogether independent of the laws that ought to rule (but don't) the price of bread. A gentleman once remonstrated with a west-end poulterer on his excessive charge for the birds we have been writing about, and was told by the civil dealer that the tariff was high ever since the wreck of the 'Royal Charter,' during which storm the shores were strewn with the bodies of the *Scolopax rusticola*. We dare say this was just as good a reason as could have been given.

CHAPTER II.

GROUSE SHOOTING.

ON no account begin shooting before nine o'clock in the morning. Birds should always be allowed to have their breakfasts, and settle down quietly for the day undisturbed, and as at the beginning of the season one can shoot on until seven at night, the greatest glutton for hard work ought to be satisfied. The last two hours of the day are often the best, the birds lying better than in the full heat of noon. It is a good rule never to go out grouse shooting in very stormy weather, as it is impossible to make a respectable bag on such a day, and any disturbance to the birds then renders them very wild, and makes them pack earlier than they would otherwise do. They are restless and suspicious in bad weather, sitting on the tops of the little knolls with outstretched necks, ready to fly away at the least attempt to approach them. At the beginning of the season, grouse are as easy to shoot as young partridges are on the

1st of September, but after a fortnight is past, they prove very wary. An old cock will rise into a "high-cuck-cuck," double, like a snipe, fly close to the heather, so as to take advantage of every inequality of the ground to shelter himself in his flight, and very satisfactory it is to lay him low. In shooting to dogs late in the season, always look well ahead of them when they have found game. A rise will then be seldom got under forty yards, and an instant lost means a bird gone away. Probably the birds will rise twenty yards in front of the dog, and about that distance in front your eyes should be fixed as you walk up ; if the birds do happen to lie closer, you will have plenty of time to bring the eye back to them ; but if they get up wild, it is of the utmost consequence that both eye and gun should be on them as they rise.

Silence is very desirable in all kinds of shooting, although grouse are less alarmed by the human voice than most other birds. Roaring and bawling at the dogs will put every partridge out of a turnip field, but will have little effect upon grouse ; still this is no excuse for a habit that is unsportsmanlike and unpleasant to your companion in the field. We say companion, because in all open shooting we hold by the proverb, " two are company, three are none." If the moor is large enough for more than two guns, the party should divide.

On the moors in the west of Scotland, where grouse are thinly scattered, they shift about according to the wind and weather, so that local knowledge is invaluable in making a good bag. Of course, with a strong breeze blowing, the grouse will be found usually on the sheltered sides of the hills, and if stormy weather has made them wild, the best chance of securing your game lies in beating the most broken ground, where you can come suddenly upon the birds round knolls, or by the sides of gullies. In many places on the east coast grouse are as thick as sparrows in a rick-yard, and they lie so close at the beginning of the season that shooting becomes monotonous, particularly as they are seldom relieved by any other sort of game. However, even then, after they have been shot at for a fortnight, and if the weather has been at all broken, they pack, and are no longer approachable. Driving is then the only resource ; for this a perfect knowledge of the country and the habits of the birds is absolutely necessary. The keeper will know to a very few yards the line of flight of the different packs, and as you walk the ground with the dogs at the beginning of the season, he should carefully point out the proper position for the guns in the several drives, and how those positions are to be reached ; beginning with the first drive after leaving the lodge, and so on to the succeeding stands, so that when the time comes for driving, you will know exactly where to go and what to do, and will be able to dispense with the guidance of the keeper, leaving him to devote his whole attention to the management of the drive, in the happy conviction that he can depend upon the guns being in their exact places, and not, as sometimes happens, a mile away from where they were expected to be. There is a great charm about grouse driving, which probably arises from the lazy vagabond way of wandering over the moor, after the steady, serious,

N

business-like plodding behind the dogs. With breakfast over, and the cigars alight, the first beat is arranged, and an hour's start given to the two guns to get into their first position. They stroll together unattended, with only a retriever at their heels, not anxiously beating for game, but with gun on shoulder, chatting pleasantly, down by the side of the burn where the water-ouzels flit. Then up a gully, by a circuitous route to the crest of the gap between two hills. Here they take up their places behind a rock, or a stack of peat, or in a bog-hole, as much out of sight as possible, and about fifty yards below the crest of the hill, so that the coming pack cannot see the guns until over the crest, when it is too late to turn. Arrived at the stands, there is time for a ten minutes' rest before the birds begin to come, so, after a thimbleful of whisky, to prevent a chill, you throw yourself upon the heather, and peering into it, watch the multitude of living things as they come and go through the miniature tangled forest. One or two single birds fly over, offering fair shots, the keeper's "Mark!" comes faintly down the wind, and in another moment a rush of wings, and a whole cloud of grouse are come and gone, barely giving time for you to place your two barrels ; then a few more single birds; and the keeper arrives to count the slain. But who shall count the wounded birds gone away ? This is the great drawback to driving, as it is simply impossible when a big pack comes over, so to pick out your bird as to avoid wounding others. In the west highlands driving is not common. Indeed, there are seldom enough grouse to make it desirable. But there, the variety of game is much greater ; black-cock, snipe, ptarmigan, woodcock and duck, add their charms to the day's bag, and we know nothing more satisfactory than laying low a cunning old black-cock, whether he be killed on a stook of corn after a long and careful stalk, or be dropped upon suddenly in a gully amongst birch-scrub and bracken. We would give one word of warning, anent the corn stooks, for it is on them that most of the poaching is carried on. Into them gather both grouse and black game at morning and afternoon feeding time, and upon them

N 2

the poacher sets his wires ; lying hid behind a
dyke, he watches the birds flock in to feed, and
as they peck the corn and are caught by the
neck in the wires, they crawl after a struggle or
two, in among the corn ; then out comes the
poacher to secure the victims and to reset his
snares.   It is a most deadly system of poach-
ing, and should be carefully watched for.   As
to the ordinary gun-poking poacher, if the
sportsman and his keeper are on good terms
with the shepherds, there is little to fear from
him.   No one could possibly shoot on the
hills, without being seen by the shepherds, and
be it remembered the shepherds have at their
mercy all the nests, and all the keepers' traps.
One moment's consideration will show how
necessary it is to have a good understanding
with these men, who are generally honest, in-
telligent, and well-educated, and by no means to
be confounded with the boors on an English
farm, nor are they to be bribed by a half-crown
pitched at their feet.   Indeed, we should
strongly advise any one not gifted with great
agility to refrain from the attempt.

CHAPTER III.

WILD-FOWL SHOOTING.

THERE is a certain property and chattel interest in partridge and in pheasants, which tends to deprive the sport of shooting them of the relish that comes of bagging their wilder relatives. The true savage instincts of our nature are not sufficiently exercised in the pursuit of birds, whose habits are almost as familiar as those of domesticated poultry. The man, however, who has a taste for genuine wild-fowl shooting, and who possesses the courage of his ideas, at once abandons himself to solitude and hardships. It is necessary for his due enjoyment and appreciation of the work to which he is devoted that he should be alone and unassisted. Let him cast about for the quarters which he intends to beat, and, having fixed on them, he must organize a plan of campaign regulated by the presumed or traditionary possibilities of the district. A fen into whose first trench the salt water oozes from a long foreshore; the plain inside stretches away for miles with here and there islands of thick-growing rush or of osiers or willows, with ponds scattered throughout, and a coarse poor grass growing over the black mould : at its farthest run from the sea rises an upland of heath-covered hillocks. A desolate landscape enough, and yet full of promise for the wild-fowl shooter.

He should be furnished with a gun of long range and a well-trained retriever, who will not refuse on occasions to face even the white horses of the sea in securing a cripple who has taken to the water. He must also be provided with a variety of cartridges, and will generally find it useful to have a different-sized shot in each barrel; for a great part of the interest and ex-citement of this sport consists in the unexpected character and dimensions of the quarry that may be flushed. Say you glance over the fen of a bright October morning. The thin hoar frost is melting away in circling wreaths, and from the call of the watchful curlew high in air you would learn that the tide is at its full, even if you did not hear the sullen close boom of the waves. You decide on walking by the dykes, and picking up whatever fortune may send in the ramble. If the dyke is free in its centre from water plants or weeds, it is advisable to steal softly to the bank and glance up and down its course, being careful to keep the dog at heel, who will make a snuffling noise from mingled pleasure and anxiety at this hour. When you have reached the bank it is quite possible that you may see a wild duck or a batch of teal dabbling about. Should you be lucky enough to catch a glimpse of them, retire from the edge of the trench and run down the fen until you arrive opposite their moorings. A rush for it is the next step, and as the frightened birds quack and clutter out of the water, let us hope hand, nerve, and eye will be equal to the occasion. Your retriever may now be permitted to scamper on, unless, indeed, you have some favourite snipe marshes in the neighbourhood. If you have, it is quite a matter of whim with these eccentric birds whether they will wait for you to walk them up in ones and twos, or whether they will spring in a wisp or ball from the bottom and burst, as it were, in all directions over your head. If there is a slight frost, they are the more likely to behave in the latter style. If a Jack is not beneath your notice, you are sure to find a couple or so of the family remaining after the departure of their more cautious cousins. Your retriever should have a nose, and be trained to point or set as well as to fetch and carry. Make him search the marsh thoroughly. That little brown bird with the drooping legs that you have just missed is a water-rail, familiarly believed by the rustics to be the winter disguise of the corn-craik, who performs odd music on July evenings in the meadows. Not far from the bog is a miserable attempt at agriculture, which has resulted in a thin eruption of dropsical turnips, set in what looks like a carpet of green chick-weed. Here is a sure find for a quail. Remember, when the quail springs, making a wonderful hubbub for its size, that you take your time and be sure to cover the bird accurately. The quail is a very small mark, has a rapid straight flight, and is constantly missed through haste.

Loading your gun, and adjusting your bag

on your shoulder, so as to swing it free of your working arm, you catch a glimpse of a strangely-shaped cloud over the hill on the edge of the fen. Experience saves you from speculating on it in the shifty manner of Polonius. There is no doubt that the cloud is nothing more nor less than army of golden plover. This army has a sort of Uhlan detachment, whose business it is to reconnoitre, and so the sooner an ambush is sought by you the better. If you are an expert, you hide in the first clump of rushes you can find, pucker your lips together, and whistle a querulous high call. If this is answered, continue to whistle, and, when the responses grow louder and louder, you must be ingenious and strong-winded enough to increase the emphasis of your performance proportionately. The Uhlan plover division does not number usually more than six or eight birds, while the main army may be counted in thousands. It is not often, indeed, that the wild-fowl shooter gets an opening into the vast squadron, the winnowing of whose wings resembles the rush of a small cataract. The slightest premature move

on his part, a single whisk of his dog's tail,
and the birds will swerve out of range, as if
with a single and perfectly simultaneous im-
pulse, whistling and careering higher and
higher, until they are beyond sight and hear-
ing. They are accompanied not only by the
vigilant vanguard of their own tribe, but by
flank brigades of the green plover or peewit—
a bird with a uniform of a completely different
pattern, and with movements of loose array,
which contrast remarkably with the parade pre-
cision of the golden plover. The peewits, how-
ever, are watchful, and more keen-sighted than
their associates. They fly slower, now and
again tumbling like tumbler pigeons in a gay,
gleeful mode. They are by no means as good
to eat as the others, and, somehow, are almost
disagreeably tenacious of life as a starling or
a wood pigeon. If you only maim them, you
have to put them through a course of killing of
which I shall spare my readers the description.
As a piece of plover-shooting strategy, it is a
paying device to erect mounds in those portions
of the fen which, from time immemorial, are
the haunts or resorts of the birds. You may

make them of peat, or you may dig a hole in the ground and get into it, or collect a bundle of rushes and nestle behind it. If the birds are pitched when you see them (and it requires practised eyes to distinguish them), if you notice them standing perfectly still, you may be assured there is no use whatever in trying to get nearer. If they are running about, it is a proof that they are not heeding you. It often happens that in these fens a race of amphibious human bipeds, when the ague allows them, come to pick up osiers, withies, or fuel, and the birds grow quite accustomed to their appearance. 'You may bribe one of these creatures to be your stalking-horse, and in this way surprise the birds, who very quickly, however, grow too cunning for the success of the stratagem.

In blustry storm weather, with a strong wind blowing from the sea, when the tide is at its ebb, leaving exposed some miles of shingle, of sand, and of low black rocks, a bag of wild-fowl may be had of the most curious variety. On such days the shore will be covered with screaming gulls, with swarms of sand-pipers, sea-larks, red shank, grey plover, cormorants, widgeon, seapie, and curlew. If the breeze comes from the north, and is moreover freighted with drifts and gusts of sleet, so much the better. You may often advance on your prey wrapped in a winding-sheet of powdery hail, and, indeed, the birds get apparently confused in these seasons of exceptional severity, and blunder within range in the most sudden and unexpected manner. Of course you do not fire at gulls, but sea-lark are not to be despised in a crust cover containing a few slices of fresh beef, a sprig of borage, some eggs, and a dash of white-wine sauce. The curlew is almost un-approachable itself, and will detect the fowler through every disguise. The 'whaup' is not content with saving itself, but will warn the other birds of your manœuvres with a cry of emphatic meaning. The curlew has a powerful note, and seems to be able to vary the key at will, so as to communicate definite intelligence to its companions. The melancholy, drear desolation of a long shore on a wild autumn afternoon, is impressively marked by the in-tensely sorrowful clang of the different waders and divers. Over the grey leaden sea you will occasionally notice a cloud of intense blackness, and against it the wings of the gulls flashing like light, while in the sough of the wind you catch a thousand plaintive whines and shrilly signals, and the stertorous grunting of the herons who have been disturbed from their fishing quarters. The fowler will find it hard to see the only birds good for his bag, unless he watches the level immediately over the ever-coming waves. He must select an hour when the most distant rocks are being gradually covered, and then the widgeon and, it may be, the wild geese keep retreating before the tide in extended straggling order, flying so low that they almost flap the water. In a stiff breeze —a storm is still preferable—there is a fair chance of having a shot even without shelter. Eley's wire cartridges, though now perhaps a little out of date, will be found useful ammunition on such a service as we are endeavouring to describe. The present writer has brought down a wild swan at thirty yards, in a strong cross wind, with a wire cartridge fired from an ordinary muzzle-loading gun. Neither your wild swan nor your wild goose is a gastronomic prize. The barnacle is supposed, by simple people, (and Professor Max Müller has been at considerable pains to account for the odd tradition), to be developed out of the fishy parasite of the same name, and any one who has ever tried to eat the bird can well understand how it came to be associated with so odd a progenitor. The wild swan combines in its flesh the fragrance and delicacy of a retired he-goat, with a smack of train-oil and red herring. Still, the wild swan is now comparatively as rare as his black brother was described to be in the familiar quotation, and is, therefore, slain for show; and, somehow or other, the goose is always regarded with an expectancy connected with seasoning and powerful sauces that is never realized. Sit down to this bird after the most skilful cook has been operating on it, and you will be forcibly reminded of that chapter in Smollett, on the " Feast after the Manner of the Ancients." The widgeon, even in rough weather, often ride over the shallows, and it is just possible to have a shot at them by creeping on hands and knees for, say half a mile, over seaweed and sand and gravel. The result of the stratagem, however, generally is that just as you are bringing your gun to bear, the villain curlew, who has been watching your every stir for the last twenty minutes, sounds the alarm, and the widgeon are up and away in an instant. The grey plover—a bird not so good as the golden plover, but still not to be despised—is also an *habitué* of the locality. The grey plover is difficult to see among the stones, and the ground should be carefully studied, not only with the naked eye, but, if feasible, with a field-glass. The flocks or stands are not so large as those of the golden plover, yet you seldom find them under three or four hundred in rank and file.

To the enthusiastic wild-fowl shooter the night is often a profitable and pleasant season for the pursuit of sport. You must get your almanac, and see that the moon will be in a position to help you in a nocturnal attack on the wild duck. As soon as the dusk sets in and the stars creep out, and the tide appears as if to snore, the wild duck come over the sea to the fen, and pitch in the pools and ponds and in the dykes.   The shooter must select a part close to a sheet of water on which the moonlight shines. If there is ho natural cover near the spot, he should have a bundle of straw thrown down by it in the day time, or, better still, a hole dug in the peat, a barrel put into it, and the cask lined with dry hay.   Into this nest you retire, and wait for duck-flight.   Even then the inevitable curlew will take a start out of you, by giving you a piece of his mind from the dark in which he is now hovering, for the express purpose, apparently, of rendering your labour in vain. You will also hear and see the snipe with outstretched wings bleating and skirling quite close to you.   The big bird sailing now and again backwards and forwards on the marsh is the supper-hunting owl, who lives in an ivied wall miles away—near the farmhouse where the solitary light sparkles, and from which a dunghill cock, of unnatural habits, shouts an untimely drunken sort of stave. Then there are intervals of the most profound stillness, when suddenly the " tingling " silence is broken in upon by a soft splash in the water, then another, then a series of splashes, then a patter as of a fall of heavy rain, and there are your ducks covering the whole surface of the pool! For a minute or two the birds are motionless ; then they commence to make inquiries, apparently, of each other before proceeding to wallow and gobble and chuckle after the fashion of their tamer kind. What a noise the gun makes !—bang! bang! right and left ; and how all the fen seems to wake up and protest against the outrage !—curlew first, and plover and snipe ; while the ducks, with a few frightened quacks, leave their dead and wounded comrades, and are out of sight in a second. Rheumatism and ague may be the avengers of the slaughtered fowl, and you are followed to your very lodge door by the warning of the everlasting curlew, whom you can even hear proclaiming your misdeeds with his "O yes! O yes!" over the waste as you rest your head on your pillow for the night.

CHAPTER IV.

PARTRIDGE SHOOTING.

PARTRIDGE shooting is at best a tame description of sport, suitable for gentlemen who like shooting-made-easy, and who take a certain pleasure in cultivating coveys, in order to have game to hand. There is seldom much excitement or science in this pursuit, and the man must be a bad performer with the gun, indeed, who cannot give a good account of his cartridges after coming out of a turnip preserve. The birds are now bred in such quantities, that they occasionally rise in flocks, covey after covey, and late in the season, unbroken squadrons may be seen starting, whirring as wildly as plover across the country. Under such circumstances alone do we believe "driving," as it is called, to be admissible. Nor can the modern system of dispensing with the dog in other ways be contemplated without regret. I sincerely wish the journals technically interested in maintaining sport would raise their voices against walking up and beating up partridge. What would old Hawker say to the practice of standing in a corner to blaze at whole flights of birds rising as thick as a cloud of starling from the turnips?

More than half the pleasure of partridge shooting lies in hunting the birds, and in watching the performances of the dogs. Followed in such a fashion the day admits of many relatively pleasant comedies, surprises, regrets, and triumphs. Here the dogs are tremendously eager and busy, sniffing and snuffing madly ; at length one crouches down as stiff as marble, backed by the companion searcher. An interval of awful suspense. This is surely the big lot farmer has seen " every morning regular" on the spot—and away flops a solitary quail, to the disgust of everybody. Ten to one you fire below the bird, or if you hit him, knock his soft body into a mere warm pulp of blood and feathers. The "Frenchmen" are to be dreaded, and it is a pity we have so many of them amongst us. They give the pointers and setters habits of poking which are difficult to eradicate, and also teach them the nasty trick of running in close upon a covey so as to startle it prematurely. The red-legs are very cunning, and prefer at any time using their shanks to their wings, and stealing through and over hedges, and in a divided and designed disorder, to the utter bewilderment of men and dogs. Opinions differ about them, but there are many reasons for their extermination, and one certainly is the bad language they provoke from shooters of a warm and impatient temper.

Partridges, as a rule, are easy birds to shoot; but then the situation and other conditions often give a variety to the mark. For instance, they may rise a good distance off, or close to a hedge, when they are pretty sure to take it in a sort of flying jump, or get up singly in lots, or all at once. Sometimes, too, they start from the centre of a stubble close as a ball, and then burst as it were in all directions. The great matter in partridge shooting is to be decisive and unflurried. Fire at the bird that first catches the sight, never taking the eye from him until the trigger is pulled.

When a covey springs at any distance between the sportsman and twenty yards, a brace ought to be brought down. It is cruel, however, to attempt the feat at long odds; as by the time the second barrel has despatched its messengers, the bird may be so far ahead as to be only wounded, or the shot may be scattered so as to maim a couple of birds, who can just wriggle out of view to die a lingering death by the side of a ditch. Much has been said about the system of modern agriculture interfering with this sport, shaving the stubbles, removing hedges, etc.; but there are plenty of birds—if not too many—when all this has been said. I am more concerned for the dogs, who, if partridges are to be " driven," might as well be tied up altogether. By the way, some one, a few years ago, suggested shoeing pointers, the modern stubble being so short as to pierce the feet, and render the dogs lame after a few days' work. This might be done, perhaps, without impeding the action of the dog, and an encasement at the same time for the lash of his tail would be no harm. The setter is naturally better protected, and it is anything but a pleasant sight to see poor Ponto at the close of the evening walking at heel as if treading upon burning ploughshares, while the the tip of his tail bears painful traces of having been in the wars. We wonder whether his ancestors were hardier in this latter respect, as old writers seldom, if ever, allude to the circumstance. No doubt the dog has softened and degenerated, somewhat like his masters; and as Thackeray said of poverty, it so far resembles death as to set in at the extremities, the hat, shoes, and gloves going first; so the pointer has become effeminate in his legs and his tail, and indeed weak in his nose, if we are to believe the annals of his olfactory deeds as chronicled in ancient records.

CHAPTER V.

SNIPE SHOOTING.

I HAVE so frequently referred to snipe shooting throughout this little book, that it is scarce necessary for me to speak of it here. A few practical hints may not be, however, out of place. Use No. 9 shot for snipe, except in windy weather, when No. 7 will be found preferable. Practice snap firing at the birds, the flight is far more diffused and uncertain at thirty yards than at ten, and you ought to be able to bring down your bird on an average between fifteen and twenty-five yards. Snipe are seldom found singly, be ready with your second barrel. On soft, foggy days, they lie very close, and require to be carefully sought for. I myself, have always used an old sensible pottering pointer for snipe shooting. In windy weather the birds are wild, and difficult to approach. In very wet weather, when the marshes are soaked, and in parts glazed as it were with water, the snipe are exceedingly wary, and when one is flushed the " bleat " will send up

hundreds after him.   They often flock under
these circumstances, and may be seen wheel-
ing in the air at an immense length.   They
seldom pitch in the same place the same day
if once disturbed, but are pretty sure to return
to it during the night.   In frost, the snipe
seek the unfrozen springs and the banks of the
brooks.   December is usually the best month
for snipe shooting.   If the winter be severe,
the birds are soon reduced to osteological
specimens, and are scarce worth bagging.
Late in the year (in February and March), they
will be found near the coast, and frequenting
wet turnip fields and grass lands.   The jack-
snipe is a cunning little creature, and will lie
at your very feet and escape notice, unless you
are accompanied by a dog.

The snipe sometimes forsakes the bogs and
moors for the comparatively dry heather and
ferns of the hills, but you will invariably find
traces of moisture in their haunts.   When in
the heather, the snipe is more cautious and
alert than in the low lands.   This, however,
to a considerable extent depends on the weather.

Never allow yourself to be hurried or flustered in snipe shooting. If you begin the day badly, you are likely to go on in the same fashion. On the other hand, if you are cool and in sound form, after making a clean score of five or six out of seven, you acquire confidence enough to be certain of doing your work creditably. Snipe test a man's aim thoroughly. The birds should be killed completely and assuredly at fifty yards by a practitioner, but near shots are the most secure, and should be the most frequent. Crossing shots at snipe are the simplest, but the knack of stopping a bird darting straight off should be learned by every one desirous of becoming accomplished in the craft.

CHAPTER VI.

THE INFLUENCE OF WEATHER ON SHOOTING.

ONE of the most essential branches of a sportsman's education is necessarily a knowledge of the habits and haunts of birds, and to render him accurate in this direction he should carefully observe the changes in the system of living amongst fowl produced by the different variations of climate and weather. In wild-fowl sport, it is of the greatest consequence to be thoroughly acquainted with the effect of atmospheric alterations. Take snipe, for instance. As a rule, they are to be found in the wet moors and marshes. They frequent the springs of the bogs and fens, or the short reeds on the banks of a shoaling lake. During a hard frost, however, they shift their quarters to the ditches with running streams, and to the green oases in the heather wastes which denote a stirring fount under the surface by which the spots are softened for the long bill of the bird. Woodcock, when the frost holds, leave the woods and coverts for the most out of the way and improbable places. I shot three brace from the hedgerows within one mile of a large town, and the same day had beaten a close preserve for them without putting up a single bird. It has always seemed to me that frost not only made wild fowl shift their residences or feeding grounds, but also rendered them stupid and bewildered. Snipe fly easiest in freezing weather I am convinced. I have met them also in small parties of four or five, blundering about the country and offering a chance shot as though they were being driven, a circumstance which I have never known to occur save during a time of snow. The wild duck, both the mallard tribe and the teal, lie close in the sedges in the same season; but, perhaps, the most diverting fun is to be had with the plover, green and golden. The latter birds are wonderfully conservative in their haunts; the frost does not find them unprepared, inasmuch as they will appear to have marked out beforehand the place to go to when the earth is white and ironbound. For years they will return to a particular field on a particular hill, as though each successive division of their vast armies had communicated the situation of the locality one to another. I have gone to such favoured spots with a perfect certainty of seeing a wary squadron either on foot or wheeling with all sorts of eccentric but beautiful curves in the sky overhead. There are indeed few sights prettier than the movements of a plover army. It sometimes consists of both golden and green together. They hold as it were a sort of review in the endless fields of the air. The lapwing wheel and lop about with the freedom of irregular horse. The golden plover are as symmetrical and as well dressed in line and form as a regiment of household troops. The lapwings do not keep silence in the ranks, for through the keen frosty air you can catch the odd petulant squeak which is so different from the clear pipe of their companions. Now is the time to steal under a hedge and whistle a call in answer to the trebles above. If you have a musical ear, the natural instrument will serve you far better than the mechanical lure. If you hear a response, do not be disappointed on looking up to see the birds sailing away as though they never intended to return. They start off on a system which I have frequently noted. They seldom, in fact, drop right down from a height, but descend in wide-ringed circles. In any other save frosty weather, I could scarce ever get a shot at these birds.

When the wind is in the east, a cutting wind with a whiff from the north in it, coming on late in the season, search turnip and potato fields on the edges of the moors as carefully as you would the moors themselves. Should the ground be close to the seashore, and this wind bearing in on the land, look sharp for wild duck in the drains. In ordinary weather they would have fled out towards the waters until dusk; this east wind keeps them back. But it makes the snipe as wild as hawks, as swift as swallows, and thins them as though they filled their bellies with it, and with nothing else. It is strange that the snipe will dwindle in Mr. Kingsley's hard grey weather, but on the first touch of frost his appetite is awakened, and he gains an aldermanic plumpness in a very short period. Mind, I say the "first" touch of frost, for should the frost continue a couple of weeks, the snipe is but the shadow of its former substance, as much changed from its original condition as a French pig differs from an English one.

If you do not despise curlew they are perhaps less difficult to come at with the wind from the east or north-east than at other times; but there is no bird so hard to circumvent as the curlew. And he will not be content with taking himself out of your reach, he will call out of danger every bird feeding within a quarter of a mile of you. The best method of outwitting the curlew is to take a note of his goings to and fro. Have him startled somewhat prematurely by a confederate, and pot him if you can from some well-concealed ambush in his line of flight. By disturbing him at his meals instead of waiting till he concludes, you will surprise him into flying low. Remember, when you jump up, to cover him instantly ; he will dart aside from a gun like a snipe. There are some men who can call curlew, but curlew language is far more complicated than that of plover, and attempting it as rule will only serve to give a warning to the most cautious of fen birds.

Now, as to shooting, say in rain. Don't shoot in rain ; it never pays. If you should be enthusiast enough to go in pursuit of snipe in a heavy shower, it may be useful to recollect that they will run around you and from you like so many red-legged partridges sooner than rise. Your unfortunate pointer, should you use one, will be puzzled enough to find the scent, and the result is that you walk over quantities of birds. The discomfort and inconveniences attendant upon sport when rain is falling heavily to my mind are never compensated for by the bags made.

I do not think this topic of the effect of the weather on birds has been adequately treated by writers on sporting subjects. The merest outline of the notion is sketched here, and was suggested to me by the singular consequences of a few days' frost upon the district which I have opportunity of travelling over. Storms over night have, I noted, the effect of rendering snipe and woodcock wild the next day, while they have a contrary influence on duck. We all know how important the discoveries of the barometer and thermometer may be to the angler. He can in some measure at least make a proximate guess as to his luck by a glance at the state of the weather. In wild-fowl shooting the elements are perhaps not so important, but they are very nearly so. A shooter may have his good and his bad day as well as the fisherman and both should be prepared for the special obstacles they may have to overcome. For instance, the size of shot to be carried, the class and character of dog to be used, may have to be considered with reference to the state of the weather, and the consequent flight, the shyness, or the reverse of the birds. It is a knowledge of details such as these that tends to make shooting an art, and which should distinguish it from the mere business of the gamekeeper. A knowledge of the nature of the soil is directly serviceable to the naturalists, for whom, indeed, the sportsman should always act as a pioneer, contributing to the stock of science as many new facts as he can pick up in his rambles with a gun. I have no doubt but that the meteorological changes which this climate has said to have definitely undergone within the last fifty years must have had a most important effect upon the marked diminution of wild fowl, a diminution as distinct and as destructive as that which has been attributed to the draining of waste lands and the making of railroads.

CHAPTER VII.

PLOVER SHOOTING.

FOR those who do not hunger after the destruction of birds brought up by hand, and who prefer a chance bag procured with some labour to a cartload of pheasants, plover shooting is an attractive sport. Unlike the pursuit of the snipe, it does not require for its full enjoyment the companionship of a dog. On the contrary, a dog has no business to do in this chase. All you require is great patience, a knowledge of the flight and settlements of the " stands," and an eye to take advantage of every natural ambush. The plover are the wariest of birds. In fine weather they are almost unapproachable. You may see them, with the aid of a field-glass, feeding amongst the stones and heather on the side of a mountain, but invariably in such an open space that the sentinels can survey the ground thoroughly. The only chance—and it can only be availed of early in the season, when the birds are not much shot at—is to have bundles of straw or

P

faggots previously planted about the spot, say the night before you intend to go out. Creeping from one to the other like a deer-stalker, and wearing grey clothes, you may manage to fire a right and left into the "stand." As long as the birds are running about and feeding, it is certain that they do not hear the fowler or know of his vicinity, but the moment they stop and remain as fixed and steady as stones, it is equally certain that they fear danger. At this instant a "rush" is about the very best thing to be done. Say you are ninety yards off; start up suddenly with the gun on full cock, and the birds are often so startled by this stratagem as to remain on the ground a few seconds. Fire one barrel at some particular bird in the centre of the phalanx, and lose no time in letting fly with the other as the regiment is forming. If you have a breech-loader, do not omit to charge again without delay. If you have wounded any birds, they begin to whistle and will recall, though they are miles away skirling and wheeling over the hills, their companions, who come flying into your face, and skimming the fern over the heads of the cripples.

In frosty weather plover shooting becomes a different affair. altogether.   The birds then desert their customary haunts, and frequent the low lands and the creeks for food.   It is remarkable that for years, for as far back as the oldest poacher can remember, these birds will seek not only the same district, but the same fields that they have been known to patronize. At this time you must either possess yourself of a " call," or, better still, learn the art of calling for yourself.   You see a dim speck in the air, which, after watching for a while, you note is moving and growing larger.   This is the " stand" of golden plover.   Presently a thin querulous pipe, a note which seems to come from the clouds, is heard.   You must be able to reply to this in the language of plover.   The birds are, in fact, inquiring if all is safe ; should you be accomplished enough to give the right password—a loud shrill whistle of a tone and a semitone—the piping approaches nearer and nearer, always waiting for the reply, until, at least if you have operated like an adept, down with a sudden swoop come the birds, and you avail yourself as best you can of the

situation.   It must be observed, however, that
both in frosty and in wet weather vast numbers
of plover are to be found on our coasts ; but,
although they appear to be the same in kind
as those on the mountain, they certainly are
not the same on the dish.   When on the
coast the golden plover are generally accom-
panied by the lapwing, also a species of plover,
but a bird not comparable to its relatives for
the sport it affords, or the addition it makes
to a bill of fare, unless, indeed, its eggs are
counted in the latter estimate.   Wary as the
golden plover are, the lapwing are twice as
cautious.   They will give a queer squeak or
bleat of warning to the former, resembling no
other noise made by a bird that we know of.
To approach plover on the coast a duck punt
is almost indispensable, and we should also re-
commend a duck gun charged with number
six.   Two fowlers are better than one in this
case, as the birds, when fired at, are almost
sure to make a cast for the land, and a chance
is then presented to a second gun stationed
behind some fen, ditch, or dyke.   Of course
the second gun should be the more convenient

shoulder-piece. And here we may note, that for this class of shooting the superior advantages of the breech-loader over the muzzle-loader are not at all obvious. The breech-loader is of service when birds are being lured by the cripples, and you must be prepared for very quick firing; but in all the other vicissitudes of the pursuit the muzzle-loader seems to tell better. For example, Eley's wire cartridges are invaluable for plover shooting; yet, most men would hesitate to use them constantly from a breech-loader. This, however, is a vexed controversy, on which much has been, and will be, said on both sides.

The greater quantity of plover supplied to the markets are probably netted. The regular "haunts" of the birds, their conservative habits, render them a prey to this kind of poaching. Those hawked about the streets in baskets will usually be found in poor company, such as the redshank, the curlew, and the seapie, instead of the grouse, the partridge, or the pheasant. The reason of this is, that they have been amongst the coast plover, and have been shot most likely by the Solent. They have a fishy taste altogether unlike the succulent, delicate flavour of the inland fowl. Plover are in perfection in November. When the bird is getting out of season, and poor eating, it becomes black on the breast, that is, the white feathers on the breast change colour. As for cooking these dainties (for dainties they are to the initiated, and quite as attractive as teal), Francatelli may have his own way of doing them, but served with fresh butter melted on them at table, a tinge of lemon, and *no* sauce, plover are not bad, especially if you have stalked and shot them yourself.

TROUT FISHING.

An Idyll of the " Wimple."

CAST I.

"CHOPIN" IN THE DUSK.

Now, between the pauses of this waltz—
played softly on the piano—a nightingale,
who is probably altogether indifferent to

it, is singing softly to himself somewhere in
the dusk.   The moon, tender and white,
shines over the smooth reaches of the Wimple,
and the breath of the roses from the clus-
tered porch, and the aromatic odour of
hyacinth comes down to me as I wave my rod,
and the line mounted with moths, over the
stream at the end of the lawn. It is in the
ripe, rich June, and the night has a velvet
muffling warmth that seems to wrap all things
in a sleepy mantle. The very stars are quiet
in the sky, not radiant or twinkling, but steady
and dim, with a dewy gelid watchfulness. The
corncrake calls from the meadow, and the mute
bat whirls for a moment in the dreamy uncer-
tain light.

As I pursue my path up the brook, the waltz
sounds faughter and fainter, the scent of the
meadowsweet and the mint appear to come
between me and it, but at moments the music
breaks through the screen of distance and the
distraction of the plants, while the Wimple
murmurs to its sedges, and the nightingale, with
short intervals of rest, continues to warble with
that luxurious affectation of not straining his

pipe, which seems to come from his knowing that he is the sole bird performer of the hour, the corncrake being only a marrowbone-and-cleaver kind of artist.

The Wimple narrows just here, and I must be careful of the marginal alders. I follow the path until I come to the broken wall of the abbey.

A big tree grows in the centre of the spot where once the hooded monks knelt at matins, at lauds, at vespers. An owl is moving above the grass-grown aisle, but ceases as I step through a gap in the broken wall, under the grim shadow of the cedar.

A statue of a Norman knight stands close by.

The wind seems to hide at the calmest and stillest hours in thick recesses of ivy. You will catch it rustling and shifting there when no other leaf is stirring.

Yes, I can still feel that Chopin's waltz has rambled from under Cousin Kate's fingers out through the drawing-room window, and into this grey ruin.

The stone crusader, who lost his hand,—not in Palestine, but on the banks of the Wimple, a few hundred years after he has been placed on his pedestal—the stone crusader, whose head is thatched with moss, and whose features have been almost washed out with rain and storm, into whose blank face or mask has passed the spirit of old-world decay to which this ground is given up—the stone crusader is a very indifferent listener to Chopin's waltz. And yet there *are* statues that seem to me to hearken very attentively to music, and the marble poetry of their dead countenances appears to glow and brighten under the influence of sound.

A glimmer of white muslin through the gap, a crisp rustle of a flounce, and Cousin Kate, the " Chopinese," as I call her, on account of her partiality for the composer, stands before me in a pretty threatening attitude. She has a red cloak over her dress, with the hood up ; and she bears a fishing-rod in her hand, for Kate is as fond of angling as I am myself.

" Well, sir, so you stole away when I thought all the time you were listening to me in the arm-chair. However, you shan't have all the fishing to yourself. What flies have you up ? I see." And Miss Kate, extracting a book from my basket, proceeded to fasten on the proper bait with a deftness which a master of our craft might envy.

" There is no use in trying now, Kate, the fish are off the feed. Look at the moon,

" Sit, Jessica."

" Bother the moon.   Do you think I came out here to flirt ?   Stand closer, unless you want to be hooked in the eye."

" You know the penalty for blinding in that case ?"

" If you don't stop I won't give you your cigars.   You forgot them in your selfish hurry to be here before me."

" In heaven's name fish away, cousin ! There, you missed a fine trout by striking in too soon, exactly what happened to you with Dick—"

Another word and a bundle of my treasured Partagas would have been flung into the Wimple.

" Now, Willie, I insist on your fishing, instead of staring at me, and fidgeting with my hood.   Twice I nearly lost my casting-line through your nonsense."

" Well, I won't any more."

" Oh, why don't you smoke or fish, or go home ?   I can take care of myself."

" Do you really wish me to go ?"

" Of course—I don't.   There, see what you have done now !   My fly is fastened in the alder."

"There, you might as well give up. I'll take the rod for you ; and here, you take my arm."

"I think you had better unscrew the rod first."

We reach the lawn garden. The lamp has only been just brought into the drawing-room, and Kate Dalrymple's Pa is still drowsing peacefully on a couch.

The nightingale has hushed, the crake has ceased, the atmosphere is quite sultry and heavy-laden with the odour of flowers. The little river purrs knowingly to itself.

Terru-terru-r-r-r—gug-gug-gug t-r-r-r-r.

Craik, Craik !

The hood is thrown back, and the pert Chopinese allows her head to nestle where it is allowed to nestle very nestlingly.

Teru-teru-gugg-gugg-terru-terru-teru.

(Confound that bird, why did he stop just as if to listen to—well, he couldn't hear it, that's a comfort ! But that wizard in the field ever so far off, how he shouts *craik, craik,* with a hoarse chuckle, as if—)

"It is a curious fact, sir," said I to Mr.

Dalrymple, as Kate handed me a cup of tea, " that poets should invariably consider the nightingale's song melancholy. The bird was so far supposed to learn in suffering what it taught in music as to wear a thorn stuck in its breast when it wished to perform."

" I believe they used to eat them in ancient Rome," returned Mr. Dalrymple, who was rather of a prosaic turn.

Kate has gone over to the window.

Gug-g-g-terru-teru-teru-r-r-r.

" It would be a shame to eat a bird that sings like that," my cousin says.

I cannot hear Philomel as steadily as I could wish, so I cross the room to the window also.

CRAIK, CRAIK.

The brute, or another of the same mood, I declare, has run up the lawn, and has rasped his instrument so loudly under the very spot where we are, that we both start and discover that we are holding each other by the hand— we didn't know it until that moment.

" Willie, why do you make me spoon so? I must play my ' Tarentelle,' and you mustn't stand near the piano."

And when this concert is over we say good-night to each other. I cannot find a fly-book I thought I left in the hall, and I am obliged to ask Kate to come down for a moment and tell me if she knows where it is.

CAST II.

LOVE AND ANGLING.

THE noon is so hot that I—that is, we—have both to give up fishing.

The golden dragonfly seems to enjoy the light upon his wings, as he quivers over the pool in which a troop of brown water-beetles are skimming and chasing in dizzy circles. From the burning cone of a poppy head travels a tiny insect, whose wings are as blue as if they were cut from a shred of the sky. The bee cools himself to silence upon a honey-suckle, the grasshopper springs his rattle in the clover. The lark is piping merrily aloft, but the landscape at the siesta hour is lulled into slumber, and its dreams are those shape-

less tender fancies that you feel in looking at
field and vale, and distant church, and mur-
muring river, and the smoke of the town that
hangs as a dim cloud far away on the hill.

"Willie, you are an inveterate dreamer.   I
don't believe you are ever really awake."

"Perhaps not; at least, in the country.   I
am dreaming very pleasantly just now, and you
are talking in my sleep."

"What nonsense!   Hadn't you better have
some luncheon?   We might then try the
poplar path where the water is shaded."

> " *The pleasantest angling is to see the fish*
> *Cut with her golden oars the silver stream,*
> *And greedily devour the treacherous bait,*
> *So angle we for Beatrice, who even now*
> *Is couched in the woodbine coverture.*"

"You were Jessica last night, you shall be
Beatrice to-day, sweet lady mine. How prosaic
of you to talk of luncheon!   Is that the neck
of a pint of Roederer, with a collar of silver
underneath?   Here, let me anchor the bottle
amongst these green water-plants, so that the
wine within may grow chill and crisp unto the
taste.   Beatrice——"

"I won't be called names out of Shakespeare. My name is Kate."

"But Kate, the prettiest Kate in Christendom,
Kate of Kate-Hall, my super dainty Kate,
For dainties are all cates, and, therefore, Kate,
Take this of me, Kate of my consolation."

"Now, Willie, I won't be teased. It is very unfair of you. And I thought we were going to be so—so agreeable to each other. You are always vexing me."

"And you are always tempting me to make you pretend to be annoyed, in order that I might have the pleasure of seeing you pout."

"Oh, dear me! What a bewildering sentence. It goes round and round, until it seems to lose its head or its meaning."

"Of course I intended it for a compliment."

"You should never attempt a thing of the kind. You do it very awkwardly."

"Not when I go to books for assistance. Give me my Shakespeare and I'll show you what you are."

"You will have an excellent opportunity for paying compliments this evening."

Q

" How ?"

" Miss Hilthorpe is coming on a visit."

" I never met her."

" You are sure to fall in love with her at first sight. Her brother, Villiers, is *such* a nice fellow."

" Indeed; and is her brother, Villiers, also expected ?"

" Yes."

I hated him on the spot, at a venture or a hazard, as Lamb says.

" You are looking cross already. I intend that you shall be jealous, so make up your mind for that."

" Then I defy you to succeed in your wicked intention. You little flirt, I'll return to town at once."

" No you won't. You would be dreadfully sorry afterwards."

" There's as good trout in——"

" Now, Willie, don't say anything rude. I shall certainly punish you for it."

" Then let us drop our foils. There's a big bank of clouds over the sun, and we may have a chance of putting an excuse for coming out into the basket."

We fish steadily towards the poplar walk, and down to where part of the Wimple is turned towards a mill-beck. You can hear the mill drumming and throbbing clearly enough.

Kate rose a fine fish.

" Throw a little above, cousin !"

The lady needs no advice on this score. Her line floats out as lightly as the threads of a gossamer that shake in the glare of a summer morning from the hedgerows. With a heavy roll and a deep suck the fly is taken, and the reel gives a sharp warning that the fish is of no mean proportions.

" Willie, you had better run out and scoop him into the landing-net, the place is full of weeds, and I am afraid of his fouling the line in them."

I step into the water. It is only a couple of feet deep, so that my virtue, if it be a virtue, of gallantry is not severely tested. Kate plays the trout skilfully towards me, and in a few moments he is tossing in the meshes. Our luck, however, is apparently exhausted by this capture. We meet with nothing for an hour,

and both begin to weary of the profitless
labour.

The Wimple crosses the main street of the
village of Wayslip. It gurgles under a grey
bridge, at the end of which is the inn of the
' Arctic Bear.' The Bear himself is standing
at the door with a screeching hen under his
arm, whose efforts to complain of certain in-
juries done to her are received with stolid un-
concern. She knows that the Bear has her eggs
in his pocket at this moment. " Would Miss
Dalrymple," he wants to say, " come in, and
rest in the parlour after her walk?" but he is
interrupted by the yelling fowl, whom he
loosens from his grasp at last, when, shaking
its feathers, it scuttles off with an ungainly
scamper. We are obliged to decline this hospi-
tality, and the Arctic Bear retires into his snug
den.

Glance over the paling where the dead in-
habitants of the parish sleep. There is a larger
population here than in the hamlet. God's
acre is thickly sown. The memorial slabs
record a singular average of longevity. A
grove of giant elms, colonized by the rooks,

shadows one side of the place; swallows are skating and scooting so close to the grass, that it is a wonder how they do not knock their heads against the tombs; and look, from yonder gate a procession enters, a coffin, the dimensions of a violin-case, it is to be put (I imagine) next a full-grown great-grandfatherly 74. The little creature within it never spoke, and knew nothing of the world which it could scarce be said to have gone out of, and yet, in the heart of that poor woman wrapped in the cloak it will be growing, day by day, a beautiful baby, more beautiful than any other she meets, an infant learning to greet her with sweet unconscious surprises, a boy, a girl, more loveable than living boys and girls. There is a myth, a kind humane fancy, that little children will blossom to maturity when transplanted above, and that the mothers who have lost them will find them again noble and strong, perfect and ready to greet those in whose bosoms they have rested even for an hour.

The violin-case is lowered away. Caw, caw, croak the sensible birds in the elms, and the churchyard is again a coursing ground and hunting field for the twittering martens who are already hawking for flies across the tiny barrow, on which the fresh sods have been laid like a blanket.

Kate has gone on before me some distance down the brown dusty road. She cares for none of these things, and is humming a gay tune, while she sticks her rod into a tree covered with yellow flowers, in order to make the roaring bees in it roar louder.

" You will be stung, if you don't mind— there !"

A fat irascible honey-maker drops cleverly on the exposed part of her wrist, and after he has taken summary vengeance for the disturbance to which he and his friends have been wantonly subjected, he tumbles on the ground.

The edge of the Wimple furnishes me with an herbalistic remedy for the sting. We are reminded by the river that we ought not to give over the trout-fishing. Besides, we must not pull up until we have paid a visit to a part of the stream to which we have given the name of Fairy Cove. Fairy Cove is a spot in which the brook broadens into a pure lakelet. This lakelet is surrounded by precipitous cliffs and woods and hills. The great cliff on the north side has its face seamed and scored by the trickling of rains, and it cannot be less than twenty feet in height. The hill is not quite so imposing, but the wood ascending from the water to an eminence of ten yards, at the very least, is impressive. The nearest approach to an eagle here is the pacific thrush or the robin, but an otter dwells in a dark cave beneath an ash tree, so that we are equipped with a wild beast. Pixies have been reported to have danced on the lakelet by the light of the stars, frisking it in and out amongst the chalice cups of the lilies, or riding in vast numbers on the back of their associate, the otter, who would, no doubt, carry them as the elephant does the cargo of children in the Zoological Gardens. You can creep out on a rock and gaze into the face of the water, until another face is revealed staring out of the cool depths. Kate and I had tried the experiment frequently, and have noted the curious inclination of the phantom heads to approach in the mirror. When looking at each other for an explanation of this phenomenon, the apparitions used to vanish, so that the whole affair, you will understand, was an optical delusion.

Our fishing for the day is concluded at Fairy Cove. Here it was, a fortnight ago, that our romance had begun. For me, it was simply the discovery in a woman's love of the hidden meaning of what I read in books, thought of over pictures, felt in music. And yet how awkwardly a man tries to express this in words! He had better not try to express it in words at all. Let him get the artists to do it for him. It may have been a vulgar fashion in old times to mark with a pencil tender and appropriate sentiments in the works of the Minerva press, but if you regard these annotations as the pathetic efforts of voiceless emotions, and impulses of souls eager for affection, to procure a hearing for themselves through the language and sentiments of others, the lead-streaks may be excused. Mary Jones, who is full of feeling, but whose grammar is defective, and whose mind is paralysed the

instant she takes a pen in hand, feels it a relief
to tell us where she paused over the sad for-
tunes of lovers in a story, and sympathized
with them. Some people should never write
their own love-letters. They should sit out a
romantic play together, go to a concert and
have their stalls side by side, visit a picture-
gallery in company. If they do not under-
stand each other afterwards, nothing will make
them, and the—you remember the close of a
song of Sir John Suckling's ? . . . Kate
Dalrymple and I used to quarrel about every-
thing but Chopin's waltz music. It was
neither very profound or severely classical, or
thoughtful perhaps, or stately, but it suited
our moods. It resembled trout-fishing, too ;
it was not very difficult, it was dainty, its melo-
dies seem to run in quaint pastoral places, it
was coquettish, it rippled on the shallows, and
rolled swiftly and brightly in the sunshine, and
Kate it was who had taught me to like it.

It was fully six o'clock when we drew near
Wimple Lodge. A carriage was drawn up be-
fore the door, and we could see Mr. Dalrymple
coming out to receive his expected guests.

CAST III.

THE CAPTURE OF BEATRICE, AND THE BOY AT THE FAIR.

I DON'T think I ever met a more disagreeable man than Villiers Hilthorpe. The fellow has been here now for five days, and he does not at all improve upon acquaintance. He has, however, improved upon his acquaintance with Miss Dalrymple to a considerable extent, but I don't care a button. She is a feather-brained jilt, just suited to play a game of flirtation with an empty-pated club-lounger. They have gone out fishing to-day. Miss Hilthorpe with them, but I refused to make one of the party.

I join Mr. Dalrymple in visiting the stables, and the dog kennels. The dogs are very well, and as far as I can see there is nothing amiss with the horses.

Mr. Dalrymple retires into what he calls his study, to look over papers. He is in fact rather bored, I believe, with my society, and as I haven't opened my mouth, except as it were upon conversational compulsion for an hour, this is not a proof of an irritable disposition.

I saunter moodily towards the back of the house, and come upon the high road. A gipsy cart goes by, and in its wake three acrobats, with greasy coats, which flap aside, and reveal the tight fleshings that expose rather than cover their limbs.

I had forgotten that there was a pleasure fair to be held beyond Lewin Park; I can return afterwards by train. Why not walk there, if only for the sake of a couple of hours' distraction? In a few minutes I am striking out a short cut for the fair, and marching stoutly under the trees of the park. I reach the crest of a hillock, and meet a very small boy, in an enormous pair of breeks, weeping as if his heart would break, by the trunk of an oak.

The breeks came up to the chin of the little man, and served him for a waistcoat; his dirty russet-apple-coloured cheeks loomed over the rim of the ill-proportioned garments, while he dug his fists into his eyes, and roared as loudly as if he knew there was some one to listen to him. He seems frightened at my first token of sympathy, which is to pull his hand from his face and ask him what is the matter. It is a sad tale altogether. Mother had given him tuppence to spend at the fair, and he let it down yon, *bohoo-bohoo*, and here he pointed vaguely to the spot where his treasure disappeared. I ventured to suggest that we might make a further search for the money; and so we did in company, and found—well, we found " tuppence " anyhow, and my proposal to conclude a pilgrimage to the fair with the now cheerful rustic was responded to with a tacit, albeit a slightly sulky compliance. But as we trudged along we grew more familiar. The urchin so far recovered his spirits as to commence performing hop, step, and jump on the grass, and to shy stones (with which his pockets were ready loaded) at birds. He was well acquainted with the route, and brought me by a short cut through a park gate into a lane, where we met a second gipsy travelling-cart, loaded with baskets and brushes, and accompanied by three yelping brats, who jeered at Little Big Breeches out of pure animal spirits. As we approached the fair field — we are amongst the earliest arrivals — Little Big Breeches pricks up his ears at the sound of a penny trumpet, and executes a saraband of delight which would do your hearts good to witness. And then at the dirty entrance what a brave show was spread for us both! The eyes of Big Breeches glistened with pleasure at the row of tents, the canvas and shed street of toys shining in the sun, the gingerbread coated with tinsel dazzling to look upon, the gay red flags, and the various notes of preparation for the fun in store for us. Big Breeches felt for his tuppence, but wasn't going to spend it in a hurry. He knew better than that. He took his fill of staring, and began to think of all the things he would like to have. Several young gentlemen of the same order and age were similarly engaged, and manfully resisted the temptations of the booth-keepers to lay out their capital on whistles and drums, or cakes. Once, indeed, I thought Big Breeches was caught. A gambling apparatus was temptingly exhibited, arranged to suit his very height, on which were placed sticks of shiny, promising sweetstuff of various sizes. The

owner of the concern when you placed a half-
penny on the board turned the table, and you
received the particular ration of sweetstuff to
which the indicator pointed.   This was the
Homburg quarter of the fair.   Big Breeches
was sorely tried, but was frightened by the ruin
of a boy who came up to try his luck.   The
boy was fascinated by the chance of winning a
yard of the prize confection which was on one
green division of the table.   He staked three-
halfpence against the bank, and though the
indicator trembled over the prize, it finally
settled above a miserable morsel, which was
handed to the winner with an attempt on the
part of the proprietor of the concern to con-
sole the unfortunate plunger with a generous
amount of brown paper to wrap his inch of
sugarstick in.   The ruined boy bore off the
parcel without looking at it, and Big Breeches
made his safe tuppence chuckle in his pouch,
and we passed on to other vanities.   After a
walk of nearly ten yards, and stopping at
everything, we met a friend of little Big
Breeches, in a white smock, holding a tiny
maiden by the hand.   The party simulta-

neously put their fingers in their mouths, in honour of me; but I turned aside to observe how the interview would be continued, unembarrassed by the presence of a stranger. Little Big Breeches was the first to speak, which he did simply by taking his tuppence out, and thereby challenged his acquaintances to a measure of their resources. Little Big Breeches seemed to have the best of the game of brag, for his friend made a kick at his shins, I suppose to prove that he had no great respect for wealth; whereupon I interfered, and proposed gingerbread all round for the company. The friends of Big Breeches neither said yea nor nay, but again returned their fingers to their mouths, accompanying me, however, to the refreshment stall. When gingerbread was over we continued our round, and now there was a delicious burst of music from an enormous peep-show, on the front of which there were, if you please, the very finest pictures that Big Breeches ever saw. Why give your penny when you could have so much for nothing? And so the organ (for why disguise it from you? it *was* an organ, and

what is more, a barrel organ) bleated a waltz,
and we stood and admired a lion devouring a
hunter (with room for the hunter and his
horse in his open jaws), and the Fat Woman
from Wales, and the cat blowing the fire with
the bellows.   And a little further on (still
within the sound of that ravishing instrument)
we gazed at the portrait of Miss Spencer, who
wears neither legs nor arms, but who, as the
bill said (which Little Big Breeches could not
read, but I could, and in this I had an advan-
tage over him perhaps), "was so gifted by the
beneficent Creator that she does all kinds of
work with her toes."   Up to this period Little
Big Breeches was stoically silent; but, arriving
at a quarter devoted to donkeys on hire, he
emitted a loud Yo-ho! directed to one of the
animals, who exhibited a slight token of being
alive.   The animal was in charge of a woman,
who, seeing the taste of Big Breeches, offered
him a ride for a penny, and then abated her
demand one half.   Paying for his pleasure
beforehand with a sigh, Little Big Breeches
mounted the ass, and was disgusted to find
that there was no galloping in the bargain, and

that he was only walked up and down a path, an object more or less of derision to a whole mob of dissipated Lilliputians who had now arrived on the green. It was with difficulty that Little Big Breeches refrained from tears, and he longed for his penitential excursion to be over. When the dame in command asked how he liked it, with the view of eliciting an advertisement, Little Big Breeches sturdily proclaimed his opinion of the entertainment, and only escaped a cuff on the ear from the virago by a clever dive out of her way.

Finding that I would require for luncheon something besides gingerbread, whelks, sugar-stick, or cocoa-nut, I retired from the fair for a few hours, making an appointment with Little Big Breeches for four o'clock, and telling him I should take him with me into the interior of the shows, whose outsides were so grand and imposing. True to my word I was back in time, and found my partner waiting for me at the gate, and so far had I gained his good graces that he offered me fully one-half a bun, which he was in the act of finishing. Now, indeed, the fun of the fair

R

had set in in very earnest! Fifty—a hundred if you like—organs playing different tunes at once, cymbals and gongs clashing and roaring, merry-go-rounds and whirligigs in full swing and freighted with little men and women crowing and screaming with pleasure, and the gingerbread fairings blazing so as to make you wink, and you will still have no idea what Little Big Breeches saw at the fair. It wasn't his first fair, he told me; but he didn't remember the other, so it was quite as good. Where shall we go first? Ah! this will suit us. A dwarf, performing canaries, and juggling—the whole for a penny, and to begin without delay. The tent is crowded with the friends, coevals, and associates of Little Big Breeches. Babies weren't forbidden; on the contrary, we made way — both little Big Breeches and I—for two of the stareingest babies in the world, who had gone into premature fits of enthusiasm merely at the lamps. A few moments of thrilling suspense, and the showman comes forward with a cage of canaries, and proceeds to make them act for us. The first canary play was a tragedy, and an executioner canary shot a bird guilty of crimes with a cannon. The audience became affected when they saw the little creature drop dead before the avenger; but the showman relieved their minds. The bold canary wasn't dead, after all; he was only making believe; and at a word from the showman, up he jumped with a twitter; and we hurrah'd, and hurrah'd again, as he hopped into his cage, and took a stiff glass of water after his exertions. The cat blowing the bellows. Little Big Breeches is roused to enthusiasm, and looks towards a baby to see how the baby is liking it, but the baby is still absorbed by the lamp, and refuses to be distracted from the contemplation of that object; but not so when the juggling commences. The juggler is a lady, a real lady, like what you see in a story-book about princesses, and not a bit like your mamma or big sisters. This real lady has feathers in her hair, and a bright blue velvet gown, and a crown of gold on her head, and cheeks of a beautiful red. The baby—two babies—applaud her with a screech, and nearly choke themselves with laughing, when she drops baby shirts out of a gentleman's hat, for

Little Big Breeches and his friends appeal to them instantly on the discovery of these articles, as a pair of nice fellows who ought to know all about them. The Dwarf rather frightened us than otherwise, and made us ashamed with his begging box. Where next, Little Big Breeches? Dogs and monkeys, wolves and bears, of course. And a little later it is time for me to go home, a place which Little Big Breeches has apparently forgotten; but he has told me where he lived and has quietly left the rest to me. Little Big Breeches is not accustomed to first-class carriages; but he goes to sleep in one, holding his new friend by the finger and a bag of fairings against the top story of his misfitting garments as if he had been a first-class traveller always. I have to rouse him up at Cranville, and we trudge together from the station to his house. It is some distance off, in a dark lane, and when the door opens there is a snug, clean little room, and the mother of Big Breeches, a comely artisan's wife, listens to my apology for the truant very amiably, and gives Little Big Breeches a mug of tea, over which I catch him

watching me as if to know how I would con-
duct myself in novel circumstances. As I am
taking my departure father comes in. He has
been looking for Little Big Breeches high and
low, as he was told to be back from the fair at
four, and it is now seven. " And thank you,
sir, for your kindness to the youngster. Here
Johnny, shake hands with the gentleman, and
bid him good night." And Little Big
Breeches shuffles over shyly enough, consider-
ing we had been so much together.

I was not back at the lodge until late. I
felt very much the better for my excursion,
which seemed to draw my thoughts away from
the one idea.

Hilthorpe was seated on an ottoman with
Kate; Mr. Dalrymple and Miss Hilthorpe were
engaged in a game of chess. I was very soon
challenged generally to relate my adventures,
and I told them with all the interest in the
chief character which I have shown above.

Hilthorpe couldn't imagine how I could
have spent eight hours dry nursing. Was
I quite sure I hadn't wheeled a perambulator
part of the time?

I was rewarded by the air of inveterate con-
tempt with which Kate listened to this elegant
badinage, but to me she scarce addressed a
word.   Miss Hilthorpe having checkmated
her slow antagonist, went to the piano, and
filled the room with Offenbach, until the room
reeked with that stuff.   The capering, jingling
tunes were thoroughly relished by the brilliant
Villiers, who was inspired by one of them, to
hum something about " piff-paff-puff," to which
Mr. Dalrymple nodded his bald head with an
air of gay fellow intelligence.

I pleaded fatigue after my long walk, and
was about to steal off, when Kate, starting up,
intercepted me at the door. " You are not
angry with me ? " she whispered ; " you mustn't
be ; " and I was brute enough to turn away
without even glancing at her in reply.

I made up my mind to return to town next
day, or at furthest the day after.

I thought the night would never pass over.
At the earliest flush of dawn I was up, and
putting my rod together, went down, perhaps
for the last time, to the ' Wimple.'

That June morning, how well I remember

it ! The dew on the grass, the lark singing with so much heart that his song seemed to rebound from the very vault of the skies, or to break as it touched it and fall in a shower of melody, the cool breath of the breeze, and the gurgling talk of the water as it ran and rippled against the sedges, they are present to me as I write with a vividness that is almost troublesome. Here is a bank after old Walton's own heart. A deep pool above a long stone slab, covered with a beard of moss, over which the Wimple runs and falls about a single foot, making a creamy swirl which ought to be a sure find for trout. I do not angle, I am afraid, with either care or skill just now. I while away an hour or two listlessly whipping the water. "Hallo! what's this?"

Making a cast into a ripple, round a big boulder, I find my line firmly caught and dragged into the air, my reel gives out, *another* reel gives out, and, as I live, I am firmly entangled.

"Oh, how tiresome!" some one exclaims from the shelter of the alders at the opposite side of the stream, and the next moment a young lady comes into sight with a decided flush of anger in her cheeks.

The witch is clothed in grey from head to boots. She has grey gloves, and grey gaiters below her short dress, a grey hat with a grey feather, but she wears her tender blush roses in her cheeks.

I was to make the advance this time, and I was in such a hurry to do it, that I stepped deliberately into the brook to cross over for the purpose.

" Now, Willie, as you are in the water, make yourself useful. Disentangle the casting lines. You were very rude last night. I was going not to speak to you again. No, stand off, and confess you have been jealous, stupid, nasty "—

" I will confess anything, only say,—"

" Say what ? "

" That you l—"

" Certainly not ; but, Willie, I never played Chopin's "Invitation" for Villiers. That is your favourite, you know, and I will never play it for any one else in the world. Do you want me to say more ? "

" No, darling, I do not."

" Then we shall be just in time for break-
fast, and you must promise me to give one of
your best boxes of cigars to Villiers Hilthorpe.
Hold this while I try and catch that tortoise-
shell butterfly ; " and in an instant the grey
gaiters were tripping through the meadow,
as though the heels of Camilla were beneath
them.

The butterfly hunter came back as swiftly
with her prize, and could not pull herself up
before she ran into the winning post. The
winning post insisted on levying a toll, and put
down the rods on the ground to avoid being
cheated.

I quite changed my mind about Hilthorpe
after breakfast. We fished the Wimple most
amicably in the afternoon, and met the ladies
at Fairy Cove for luncheon. I do not think
I need prolong this little sketch of love and
trout fishing any further.

I only wish that all honest anglers may be
as fortunate in their sport as I was upon the
Wimple, and may learn to admire the beauties
of Chopin as well as of Walton. Catholic
tastes and sympathies add to our oppor-

tunities of enjoyment, and anybody who can make love and fish at the same time, will find that " angling for Beatrice " is a diversion which enables us to cast our lines indeed in pleasant places.

A MAY IDYL.

— ◆ —

THE DARYL IN MAY.

BY A TROUT ANGLER.

HERE is an old grey bridge crossing the stream Daryl about a mile above the tideway. Though so near the coast the sea-water does not flow to this point, for the main current goes to meet the Avonbeg. It is a bright cheery morning in May. The air is full of the spring, the keen fresh spirit of growing and budding is in the atmosphere, and makes the tender, lucent leaves shiver on the trees down there in the meadow. The fields are silent and deserted. Folding from them is a white vapour which steals off and climbs the steep hills crowned with Irish fir. On a sudden the clear note of the lark is heard in the sky, and as he calls and

calls a score of voices as sweet as his own join
in the concert, and the choir of birds break in
from bush and briar as if they had not the
livelong day to spend in discussing the music
no man has taught them.   From the base of
a dead moated grange, with sightless windows,
a long-legged heron flaps lazily into flight,
giving a sort of chilly cough as he takes his
departure for a feast of small fry in the mill
beck.   Listen keenly for a moment, and be-
tween the matin chorus of the birds, the
dreamy murmurs of the river, the weird whis-
pering of the reeds, touched by the passing
wings of the wind, you can hear the great sea
rolling and booming on the sands, and looking
afar off behold the shining plain of the ocean,
and the thin phantom image of a steamer
sailing on the verge, and becoming dimmer
and dimmer every moment.

This is my first day for the season with the
rod.   I make a chair of a fishing basket, and
take out the flybook, lighting a cigar to as-
sist judgment to a lucky decision on the point
of a wren's tail or hare's ear.

How little a river changes, and how much

we do! As I glance at the glittering Daryl I seem to know every old snag and bramble in the reach before me. That venerable stone, bearded with moss, behind which there is nearly always a big trout — and when you catch him, as I hope to do, another will take his place to-morrow—that bearded old stone used to seem a rock to me when I served my apprenticeship to the art of angling with a pin. Under the elder a bit further up I have listened with the perfect faith of ten years of age to the stories of Leprecauns, told by the lying, clever, eternally lazy varlet, under whose charge I was placed during my country rambles. The fellow localized his yarns, and would point to a mound on which a dwarf in a red waistcoat and knee breeches was seen by him making brogues. The fairies are dead now. . . . I have my rod together at last, but I must wait until a cloud goes over the sun. Now, there is a momentary eclipse, and I observe, as we are passing into it, that the same effect is produced on our chanting little fowls when the veil covers the sun's face as you might note when a handkerchief is flung upon

the cage of a garrulous canary. That was a
neat cast, though I say it. The gossamer line
waves from the lithe top joint, and the quiver-
ing lure falls as deftly on the stream as a leaf
overweighted by a single dewdrop from the
flower of the monthly rose. There again is a
performance worthy a master of the craft.
Ha! he has it! The fish is a beauty, not
bigger than half a pound, if as much ; but ob-
serve the glowing garnet jewels on his back,
the rich brown and bronze in which they are
set, the gold tinge on his white belly, the
fading glint of his eye, in which the colours
alternately flash and die out, like the prisoned
light in the opal. Pluck for him a death
couch of emerald grass, of yellow primroses,
and preparing this fragrant bed in the end of
of your basket, try what you can do to find a
companion for the primal captive of your rod.
The Daryl takes a leap about a mile higher
up, and it is best to make a short cut to reach
the mimic cataract. You walk across the rich,
wet fields, and through a grove of elms, in
which a big colony of rooks are cawing over
the family affairs of the time. Mr. Herbert

Spencer tells us that the rook discusses poor and rough melodies, but that we are reconciled and indeed attached to his uncouth tones, because we hear them in pleasant seasons and pleasant places: There is, I think, besides, a homely, honest ring in the strains of the clergyman-dressed bird which is effective independent of the interest of association. Above the rookery is a mill and a forge. The forge is asleep as yet. The fire is out, the door is open, and if anybody cared to go in and steal the large bellows and a waggon wheel there is apparently nothing to prevent them. The mill, however, is at work. It churns, and grinds, and sobs—a laborious giant groaning over a heavy task. The good miller, himself, is enjoying a morning pipe on a plank which crosses the stream. He sits with his legs dangling over the water, and his arms folded, while the tobacco curls in blue wreaths around his battered straw hat. He gets up, and (we are old friends, this miller and I) proposes to bring out his own rod, and join me for a mile or two.

Although the miller fishes the water after me, I confess he picks up in a short space of

time more than I have succeeded in bagging
in two hours.   I believe I rise more trout, but
the miller is a wonderful hand at "striking,"
and if a trout only looks at his fly it is all up
with that trout.   The miller leaves me ·at the
cataract, and insists on pitching his fish into
my basket.   The Daryl. Niagara might be
about ten feet in height, and yet you would be
surprised at what a respectable pother and
noise it kicks up.   Below the fall there is a
bubbling, gurgling pool, with flecks of creamy
foam twisting round and round the tremen-
dous inner gulf of the màelstrom, in which the
wreck of a bird's nest apparently, and half a
dozen sheaves of straw are chasing each other ;
there is a tiny dab chick, who disappears the
instant you catch sight of him.   Unpack the
india-rubber coat you have brought with you
to provide for the April shower.   Watch
how it comes.   Dark nebulous islands float
together from different wastes in the sky.
Between them the intense blue is still visible ;
but they grow thicker and thicker, these ma-
jestic bergs, until the hollow of the vast cupola
is almost filled with them.   One that seems as

broad as a whole continent rises slowly up-
wards, and widens as it moves; and shortly the
masses lose individual form, and merge in a
dense flock. The westerly breeze sweeps with
a strong gust over the landscape, and brings
with it a soft, almost gelid rain. And no
sooner is this done than the sun is out again,
shining more brightly than ever, and the
clouds scatter; but the rain still falls, and the
wonderful bow of Iris appears, but only to
dissolve and glimmer for a minute. We fish
at intervals with good fortune, and by the time
we reach Glendaryl Wood our basket is
heavily freighted. The wood of Glendaryl,
through which the Daryl runs, has a mixed
congregation of trees. They are of all ages
and sizes and sorts. Old greybeards, whose
feet are swathed in lichen and mosses; tender
saplings over whose head few storms have
passed, and in whose branches birds have not
yet cared to live. There is an odour of pine
by the dim avenue we are traversing. The
wood is almost dark in the leafy summer, and
even in April there is a perpetual dusk in Glen-
daryl. Sometimes, however, you arrive at a

s

glade—a close of green grass, with an ink black pond in the centre of it. Is that the shout of the cuckoo? No; if you listen more attentively yon recognise the purring of the pigeon, "the moan of the dove in some immemorial elm," expressing the quiet brooding ecstasy of intense inarticulate love. The shower that we met has left millions of flashing diamonds on the trembling gateway of lindens, opening again into the recesses of Glendaryl. And the Daryl is quite another river here. It has a mysterious, unceasing conversation with itself, and if you stop fishing for a second, perhaps you find words for that never ending song that goes on without any. At times it gossips in a snappish, shrewish fashion with a sturdy boulder; anon it dashes down a lane of thick branches, threatening and bragging like a man who is in a passion and afraid of his enemy. You come across it in quite another mood where it glides smoothly, with just an odd word or so of greeting to a stooping willow or a friendly chuckle with a bunch of reeds, and then, grave and decorous as a hooded nun or gloomy trappist, the Daryl enters its cave. Yes, this river has an underground course for half a mile. Put your ear to the ground a hundred yards from its departure into the dark, and you might hear it, as it were, contending with angry, uncanny things, more uncomely than even the blind, ugly fish, that are supposed to dwell in the black waters. But the Daryl bursts into an open meadow outside the wood with a positive roar of relief and triumph. It takes a header over a rock, and plunges merrily along, only staying to clasp and kiss a few ancient weir-stakes beneath Croom Castle.

The evening is drawing near. The rod is unshipped; the basket freshly strewn with flowers, loaded as it is with trout to the brim. The crows are calling from brown furrowed marshes; there is a red flame in the west, but the lark still sings as if the day was young. The air is cool and feels damp. From the road we can see the winding Daryl, turned, as the poet says, to blood with the miracle beams of the great high priest, the sun. By the time we reach the bridge, where we started,

the night is announced by the pale horn of the
moon, which hangs on the ragged edge of the
hill.   There are as yet but few stars out, and the
wind is rising with a dreary soughing growl, as
though it had an uncomfortable series of duties
to perform when the world was asleep and at
rest.   Now you can hear the sea plainly enough,
and the sheen of the light-house lamp sends a
streak of narrow radiance on the weltering tide.
Everything near is being hidden more and
more from you.   The bushes by the roadside
lose their shapes and disappear; the cabins are
spirited off; but the Grange, in which Ma-
riana might have pined, stands out in relief, or
appears rather to be floating off the ground or
cast on the dark screen of the night, like a
grim picture of ruin in a magic lanthorn.
Later on, the angler might continue his sport
through these gloomy hours; but in May the
trout do not feed on late suppers.   And so,
with an appetite and a pleasant anxiety for
slippers, the fisher reaches his inn or his home
at last.   Before he sinks to sleep his mind
repeats a few of these immaterial incidents re-
corded above.   The birds have sung, the wild

flowers have blown, the rivers talked, and the clouds have come and gone for the most of us at some time or other, before London, our stony-hearted stepmother, claimed us.

MY FISHING COMPANIONS.

BY THE RIVER.

A HOT July day in the wood of Glenlawn. It is a deep and dark wood, in which there are but odd skeins of sunlight, across which you can see the insects swarming like motes in a beam. The Lawn brook is gurgling, drumming, and whispering; the pigeons are cooing overhead; now a thrush sings, now there is a profound summer silence, only broken by the constant tune of the water and the voice of a girl chanting a wild Celtic air in the fields without.

I have been lying in the moss at the foot of an oak for the last hour. There is nothing in the creel, the trout would not rise; I have tried every likely fly in the book, and I have given it up and lit a cigarette. I wish I could come across old Sam Freeman. Old Sam Freeman is a professor of the gentle craft who haunts these parts.

I watch the stream in a lazy, idle mood. Suddenly there comes a sound from out the dusk of a brake at the opposite bank—the sound of a whistle, to which the pleasantest trill of a flageolet is meaningless.

This is the overture to the approach of the accomplished Sam Freeman, who can whistle, with his mouth by the river, tunes sweeter than Pan blew from his reed.

The whistle eeases, and I know that Sam is putting up a cast—a work of so important a nature that it must not be interrupted by music.

Presently the whistle—which has an odd charm in it, as though it were an incantation—is heard again, and I can see the point of a rod moving. I am better acquainted with Sam's peculiarities than to startle him by any notice at this moment.

With what a grace and lightness the tiny line drops behind that bunch of weeds!

there is twenty years, aye, thirty years of ex-
perience in the performance. By Jove! he
has a rise, and whisk! out goes a little speckled
beauty.

"Good morrow, Sam."

"Oh! good morrow, sir, an' good luck."

"I had no luck, Sam; hold on and I will
cross over to you."

Sam is a grizzled veteran, clothed in a dun
dress, and wearing on his nose a pair of silver
spectacles. He is very proud of these spec-
tacles, as remnants of family plate; for Sam
though he ties flies and sells them, and is not
above taking half-a-crown for his offices during
a ramble, yet claims to come of a good stock,
and the spectacles are reported by him to have
belonged to his great-grandfather, who farmed
Ratheragne Grange. If you want to know
why Sam is poor, take whisky for the first rea-
son, whisky for the second. He was reclaimed
—from the grave and the poor-house that is—
by a priest, who made him "take the pledge;"
but he had long ago swallowed his few acres,
and it was fortunate for him he had a passion
for, as well as a skill in, angling.

In one respect old Sam was a nuisance. He was never refused leave to fish on his own account anywhere; and if you wanted a stream to yourself, it was almost impossible to have the solitary possession of it for a day in his neighbourhood. He had " short cuts " from one brook to another, and knew exactly when the trout were on the feed in each. It was from him I learned that the fish in the Lawn, for instance, were in the habit of rising to flies at the unusual hour of noontide in the early summer months.

" I think, sir," remarked Sam, " we had better put up a nateral (*Anglicè* the ' natural ' fly), they'll not be lively at anything else."

" Have you brought them with you, Sam ?"

" Leave me alone for that," and Sam turned round his basket, from which he produced a cow's horn plugged at one end, stopped with a cork at the other, and perforated with holes.

Raising the cork out at one corner, a large bluebottle began to make an effort for his deliverance, and to buzz for it as well as he could under the circumstances. Sam shut him up again, and proceeded to take down his flies from the casting line, substituting a long piece of gut with a single hook to it, with a grain of small shot fastened close to the hook. he takes a bluebottle as though he loves him.

"I thought the oak-fly would be better, Sam."

"Not at all, sir, not at all; have'nt half the life in him the blue-bottles have; an' besides, I catches bigger trout with the 'bottles. Let us try under the little fall beyant."

"Beyant" was half a mile, at least, through the undergrowth of briar, that sent out a sweet scent as we pressed it; through a grand avenue of foliage, that rose above us like the pillars and arches of a noble minster.

"Asy, sir! asy!" whispered Sam, who believed in the sharp hearing of trout (which I do not). "Asy, sir! and I think we ought to get something here."

The brook falls about a foot amongst a group of rocks, and bubbles and swirls into a pool, on which some snow-white flocks of foam are chasing each other.   Sam drops the 'bottle, whose legs are actively moving, into the fall, and lets him sweep into the eddies.   Down goes the point of the rod, and up comes a plump herring-size trout to our very feet, as quickly and as deftly as only an artist like Sam could bring him.

Again a 'bottle is put on, and Sam successfully repeats his performance.

After this I am furnished out by Sam with a 'bottle and the other necessary apparatus, and we fish with excellent sport down to the mill.

The Bride is known everywhere as a "sulky" river.   It has baffled anglers from all parts, but has tempted them too on the chance of having a good day on it; for a good day on the Bride is something, I can tell you, to remember.   Sam Freeman promised to find such a halcyon occasion for me.   "We must watch the strame," said Sam, "watch it by stopping at the hotel at Conna; mebbe in a week we would have an opportunity at the water thin."   And so to have an opportunity, as Sam called it, we did put up at the inn.

The "opportunity" came. A wet day, a day of warm rain with occasional outbursts of sunshine. This Bride is a very picturesque river. It runs through a vale bordered with rich meadows, from whose far edges the hills slope, the hills crowned with groves of Irish fir, in the midst of which you catch interval glimpses of white farmhouses. By the stream there are numerous old castles of the Cromwellian period, grey and battered, and ivy-covered. Under the walls of one I hooked a four-pounder, and had some tough work to land him. Sam and I had splendid sport on the " good day ;" the trout did not run very large, but the average size was very satisfactory. At the luncheon hour we sat on a block of masonry from the dismantled tower of the Saxon fortress, and Sam pointed to spots in the landscape, where the Bride flowed, and where he had killed fish of astonishing proportions.

With Sam on the Bride in August, after sundown. When we move our rods over the stream the flush has faded from the pools and reaches, the dusk steals away, one by one, tree and castle and hill from view, and lights begin to glimmer in the windows of the peaceable dwelling. We have put up moth flies, and are fishing in the shallows, to which the heavy trout come at eventide. The air is warm, and through the song of the stream I can distinctly hear the deep, amorous kind of suck that Sam makes at his dhudeen, as he watches me, rodless, but armed with the landing-net. A ghostly object sails swiftly across our faces.

"That's an owl, sir; the blayguard is lookin' for his supper."

"And quite right, too, Sam; why shouldn't he?"

"I never like to meet the like of 'em; they say 'tisn't lucky."

"Why?"

"Well, sir, I suppose it stands to rayson, you see, that bein' out all night they see things that aren't good." ("Things that aren't good"—an Irish periphrase for spectres or elves.

"Surely, Sam, you are not fool enough to believe in fairies or banshees?"

"Be gor, then, I am, sir; and by your lave

I would sooner not be talkin' of 'em just now an' we close to Sheraun berrin' ground."

And so our conversation dropped, and I tied up my rod and lit a cigar. Next morning we are up with the lark, or rather with a hundred larks, for there is a Handelian chorus of the matin singers, warbling under the blue arch of the sky, and caring little whether my ladye sleeps or not. Sam Freeman prepares our tackle while I take a plunge in the river. By the time I have made my exceedingly simple toilette he has everything in ship-shape, and away we go for an hour's fishing before breakfast. You should have seen the sour expression of Sam's face when two magpies came chattering and flirting from a willow.

"No luck for us to-day, sir!"

"Why, Sam, what with seeing owls at night and magpies by day, it is a wonder you ever catch anything!"

"I'd catch more av I didn't see 'em, sir; that's how it is."

"Well, we cannot complain this morning; a dozen already. Come, let us have a couple cooked at once."

And so to the inn, and to eat the delicate pink flesh of the fish, or fish of the fish, but by any name a delicious treat for an honest and hungry angler.

NOTES ON TROUT FISHING.

CHAPTER I.

EARLY TROUT FISHING.

ACCORDING to the best authorities on such matters, the trout is not in good condition anywhere in the month of February. There is, to be sure, an almanack or customary licence to angle at that period, but the privilege should not be enjoyed by an angler true to the nicer instincts of his sport. The experts are as dogmatic on this point as the hierarchs of every pursuit or calling are certain to be. The fact is that some rivers are far earlier in this respect than others. In large streams the family arrangements of the fish imply that they should be let alone until the season is advanced to April or to May; in smaller rivers March may be the best possible time; and in mountain brooks and lowland becks capital sport indeed may be had before the faintest tinge of green colours the bleak hedgerows.   Here, of course, you cannot expect four pounders—there is no prospect of an exciting scuffle with a plump walloping fish ; you must be content with meaner prey, with the diminutive but not less lovely fry that look so pretty in creel or dish.

Suppose you select a mountain stream for the scene of your operations.   Make it a point to go up as high on it, as near to its source as you conveniently can.   Choose a morning with a soft yellow mist for your start.   Take heed that there has been no frost overnight.   The pallid rime on grass or leaf forbodes an empty basket to the angler.   You will find what is called a fresh day, when the spring seems to make a sudden advance towards quickening the still heart of the year.   The sky is soft with woolly clouds ; the westerly tender wind is just strong enough to cause a fly from your casting line to tilt deftly over the water ; the softness of the air tempts the blackbird to chuckle in the hollies, and winter is banished

T

from the peak of the hills where the snow crown was so long laid. Every stream, writes Mr. George Macdonald, has its own song, but the mountain stream trolls its bravest chaunt in the month of March, as it rushes between the grey moss-tipped boulders full and buoyant. The call of the brook to the eager angler the first day he seeks its side, rod in hand, is wonderfully pleasant. His eye scans the favourite pools, and reaches, and heavy swirls of brown water, which twelve months back he could count upon for a " rise." The music seems as familiar in his ears as though he had never lost the tune of it, as though the record of the working world had been blotted out from his mind altogether. It is strange how completely and effectually river-sides preserve their features. There is the thorn-bush, with the nodding treacherous snag drooping over the bank, where you came to grief with your tackling before you went to college. That tiny peninsula of sparkling sand has altered neither shape nor dimensions since you can remember it as a youngster personating Walton under the ignoble difficulties of a crooked pin and a garden worm. Hence the pensive fisherman plucks an hour or two of his vanished youth out of the past as he plods along the stream in the March forenoon. But -he must not forget his business in reverie. What flies are you to put up? Any flies will do, so that they be tiny, and not too bright if the brook be clear. The March trout is not fastidious. He is no epicurean critic of the contents of that ingenious store of imitative insects you carry in your pocket. He is not used to the elaborate preparations of the shops, and for that matter he is rather ignorant of winged ephemeral food in any shape. But what you offer must be skillfully and cautiously presented. Stand far in on the bank. Watch that promising spot below the sobbing and gurgling waterfall and wait until that big island of a cloud drifts across the face of the sun. As soon as the glitter has faded from the place, twitch with that grace and lightness that become the practised hand your almost invisible line, and there—you see your fly has been taken, and a herring-sized beauty is quivering on the withered fern by you. At this hour

T 2

the big ones like to lurk under the overhanging slabs of turf, where the rotten stump of a tree diverts the slack of the rivulet, where weeds float thickly with plenty of water beneath them. You must faithfully try these several haunts with patience and with unflagging care. There are anglers who do their work like that periwigged fellow who spoiled the player's speech. Be none of these. Sport may be converted into a fine art by talent and discretion. Trout fishing is a fine art if properly carried out. Worms? Who brings his bottle or his tin casket of these abominations into the field is fit only to compete for a silver watch with bricklayers and costermongers at a Cockney fishing match. Your stream may bring you into a silent fir-scented wood. To cast with security among the overhanging trees requires considerable dexterity. You must learn to do so underhand, and what ununderhand casting is cannot be taught on paper. In the wood your path often runs upon velvet moss softer than the carpet from Turkey, and in a twilight gloom that has the odd effect of making the shout and racket of the brook much more noisy and obstreperous than it really is. Where an opening occurs you may not improbably light on the first pale "un-married" primrose you have met for the year, and on the lurking secretive violets. They make a sweet couch for a dead trout to lie upon ; and if you have a strong imagination perhaps you will find they give your fish a flavour. The wood is a still spot in the March afternoon. Pigeons clutter overhead, but have not generally begun to make love to each other, cooing like muffled French horns in an orchestra. A thrush or a blackbird pipes an occasional stave, and then ceases. The rivulet alone breaks the silence, while now and again you catch the regular beat of a mill-wheel ever so far off, but only when the brook has allowed its voice to droop to a sort of con fidential whisper as it glides quietly and darkly into a sort of tunnel composed of interlaced leafless tree branches.

There is no rule of trout angling that may not be occasionally broken with advantages Even that law so emphatically laid down in this slight sketch touching the futility of attempting to fill a creel in the frost has been violated on certain rivers without the penalty of ill-luck having been incurred by the fisherman. Nay, in a cutting wind, with showers of sleet and pattering hail sweeping wrathfully over the stream, big, profitable trout have been tempted from its half-frozen depths. But it must be admitted that angling with your teeth chattering in your head, your nose blue with the cold, and your hands numbed and raw from the inclement weather, is not an exhilarating or attractive occupation. Yet it may be had under such trying circumstances, I can assure my readers. Nor where the opportunity offers need the fisherman postpone trout catching until March or April. The fish caught even earlier may not be at their best, but they are frequently in very good condition, and those that are not, can be returned to the stream. One great advantage of early trout fishing is that you are almost certain of getting more " rises " than you will be later. The trout feed voraciously, and do not suck or frisk with the flies, but appear to bolt them with refreshing eagerness and credulity.

When May comes, and richer June, the trout often disdain to gobble the daintiest composition of silk, hair, feathers, and fur, and will tantalize you for hours by rolling over and making believe to seize your hare's ear, your wren's tail, or what not.   In March the fish are bold and inexperienced.   You must not, however, on that account trust to clumsy tackle.   Let your rod be light and springy, your casting line thin and slightly coloured, so as to take the white gleam out of it, your flies arranged to suit the dimensions and history of the brook you adventure upon.   Always bear in mind that every brook and rivulet, great and little, have their own idiosyncrasies and characteristics as far as trout are concerned. These vary with every month, and no direction or instruction applicable to one will be applicable rigidly to another which may be situated only a mile or so away.   It is, then, absolutely necessary for the angler who desires to cast his flies over strange waters to seek the advice or aid of that gaitered or booted poacher with cat-gut round his hat, who is invariably found haunting the stream.   It must be made worth this gentleman's while to permit himself to be tapped for information: if possible purchase from him at your first interview, his fly book. If you do not buy that unsavoury album at once, do not bid for it all, for in order to provide for such a contingency and windfall, and still to keep you in his power, the professional parish angler will stuff it expressly for you with his stock of fly-tying failures, should he have an opportunity and time for reflection. Never listen to his invitations to degrade you to the level of an angler who depends for his sport on the livid nastinesses of the tanyard. Should the expert avoid your solicitations, be mean enough to watch and to dodge his movements. Observe the hours he keeps by the river, and follow suit. On the whole, indeed, it may be said that anglers' guides and companions are a harmless and guileless race of mortals, who are willing to earn an honest penny in connection with their craft without any exceptional forwardness or importunity. In trout fishing in new quarters they are, for the first few days at any rate, indispensable. Afterwards, however the angler should bear in mind that his sport to be thoroughly appreciated and relished must be followed in a reserved and solitary fashion. A man should be his own best friend by the trout stream. The discipline of a spell of silence is good for most of us, and there are voices to listen to in the fields and woods by the brookside in March for those who choose to hearken to them.

CHAPTER II.

TROUT FISHING.

When the capture of trout is for the first time in the season rendered permissive by the weather, but impossible to the angler from claims or cares of business, there are few sights more distracting to the fisherman than the brave show of speckled beauties set out upon the marble slabs of the great dealers in the food in which St. Peter traded. Your sea-fish is a gaping and unsightly object. The cod looks as though he had in life been startled at some horrible wonder of the deep, and his

countenance in death wears still an expression
of fright ; the turbot is simply an expanse of
white meat, suggestive of no antecedent his-
tory ; the gurnard is as ugly as a mythological
dolphin ; the mackerel and the red mullet have
already lost their claims to a certain gaudy
attractiveness by exposure to the air.   But be-
hold the salmon, and his cousin-german, the.
trout !   The one glitters in a noble silver coat
and lies in state like a king as he is ; the other
in a russet mantle studded with rubies, or ex-
hibiting an underwaistcoat of an Ophir hue, is in
every respect worthy his distinguished relative.
And the honest angler studies him with an
eye, let us hope, that brings with it the power
of seeing beyond the limits of the fishmonger's
stall.   That three-pounder has certainly come
from a lake.   That bouquet of troutuli—if the
word may be coined—surely they have been not
long since sportive neighbours in a frolicsome
beck, in a giddy brawling burn.   They are all,
you are afraid, the victims of the net.   Until
very recently they were protected from the
angler by the floods and the frost ; for until
the time of the cuckoo and the hawthorn

buds the trout rod is often left to lie upon
the rack where it has hybernated. These little
fishes have scarce known the luxuries of gelid
water, or the full flavour of aromatic riparian
plants; for, despite natural history, we prefer
to believe, as an agreeable fancy entertained in
common with the elder brethren of our craft,
that the trout not only enjoys the scents of
spearmint and meadow-sweet which grow near
his retreats, but that, in brooks more favoured
than others with fringes of odorous and pun-
gent flora, he himself smacks of them.

There be trouts and trouts, as well as anglers
and anglers. There are monsters in the Thames
which, when a man descries, he reports as
though they were whales; and people come
from all parts attempting the capture, and dis-
pensing, as it were, with harpoons, for the sake
of sport. In a sporting paper a correspondent
writes:—" Abraham Stroud tells me there is a
very fine trout feeding between the lock and
the weir." Next week there will not be a bed
procurable at any of the inns situated near
the pasture district of this "very fine trout:"
he will have a hard time of it. Indeed, only

a big trout can hold his own in the Thames. He must have a pretty strong stomach, and a frame large enough to defy the cavernous maws of the insatiable pike. How he escapes destruction in infancy is astonishing; from his birth he is as persecuted as the children of princes were of old, and before he arrives at maturity he has gone through as many hazards as a soldier on active service. He who uses worms, who has sat in a cockney punt with baited hooks, who has entered into competition for sending down the scales with comic singers off duty at Hendon pond, will never be an angler in the true sense of the word. He is but a fisher for the pot, a mere purveyor. The artificial fly, and nothing but the fly, should be the shibboleth of the real sportsman. I should object even to the employment of the natural lure, the natural fly, oak or blue-bottle. These latter are, no doubt, tempting baits. I know that at high noon, when the sky is inflected with a cloud, when the air is not only warm but hot enough to silence the birds, to cause the cows to pant in the meadows, when the stream is shallow and clear

as crystal, the creel may be furnished by a re-
sort to living decoys. I am ashamed to
admit that I am acquainted with the manner
of doing the deed : the stealthy approach with
shortened rod to the tree that overhangs a
shadowed pool, or dark swirl round a boulder
——I know that by letting the unfortunate in-
sect (a grain of small shot may be attached
to the finest gut near the hook) gently down
on the water that—but these are demoralizing
revelations. To be sure our father, Izaak, was
an inveterate bait fisher——a dealer in singular
unguents and pastes. His was a primitive age.
We must be judged in our pastimes by more
intelligent standards. After having acquired
sound principles on the subject of trout
angling, there is more to be learned ; the
technical ethics of the pursuit do not exhaust
its mysteries. You must study the art of
casting. Clumsy men often break down at
this point. To cast a trout-fly properly
necessitates the possession of a light hand, a
calculating eye, and an absence of nervous
haste. Pelting a trout with hooks covered
with tinsel, fur, or feathers will never tend to

render your basket heavier, unless the trout be, as an Irish gamekeeper once observed to a neophyte, "a fool of a trout." The length of line left out must be proportioned not only to the size of the rod, but to the experience of the gentleman at the butt of it. The fact of the matter is, that no reading of the thousand and one authorities on the topic of fly casting, is worth a dozen lessons from an angler by the side of a stream. Trout casting cannot be learned theoretically. Rivers, too, should be specially observed, and their peculiarities carefully noted. A stranger going to a new stream should consult a local angler as to the flies that take best in it, and the favourite haunts of the larger fish. There are plenty of tempting-looking spots on a river over which a rambler will cast for ten minutes with the most sanguine expectations, and from which a fish has seldom if ever been pulled. Then there are streams in which the fish will rise in defiance of the sort of wind and weather which you have hitherto thought precluded the notion of sport. As a general rule, soft days, with medium water of a clear brown, we have found the best; yet there are rivers where, in order to do anything, you must wait for a roaring gale, for rain; and in the thick of showers the very finest fish will come up boldly to the line. Snow or frost invariably sickens and renders sulky the trout as far as artificial flies are concerned.

In midsummer the best time for sport in most rivers would be the early morning; the grey dawn, before the light glistens on line and hook, and frightens the larger trout under the banks and to the bottom of the deep holes. Rivers are so coquettish, however, that unless you have information to the contrary you may take your chance at any hour. There is a pleasure in the very uncertainty.

Trout fishing has, in some respects, advantages over salmon fishing. It is neater, cheaper —if that be a consideration with any one—and allows more opportunities for the enjoyment of landscape and reverie, the two chief pleasures of a country stroll. The trout rod is no burden, the apparatus is all together and economical. The use of it does not tax the strength. Ladies have learned how to operate with it most successfully. But the devoted trout angler never takes a lady with him. Her companionship distracts him. And then lady anglers are prone to getting caught—in the trees and the like. They must be rescued from their difficulties, and the cavalier must smile in his wading boots, as though he enjoyed it, while he marches up to his waist into the cold water to free hooks from the detaining bul-rush, bramble, or drooping ash. Trout fishing and flirting cannot be reconciled with each other in a sufficiently profitable manner ; when attempted for consecutive days by young people in the spring, their flirting contributes only to the peace of the trout.* This pursuit (we mean now trout fishing simple,) may be enjoyed in the most picturesque seasons : it may be successfully adventured at the dawn, before the dews are taken from the grass ; it may be (in deep-shaded wood glens) followed up at high noon.

You may, at the fall of the year, between the

* Of course an exception may be made when the amusements may be combined in the fashion described in the chapters of the ' Wimple.'

lights, go down to the river at dusk and put up your white moths (throwing them over the shallower reaches), what time the grey owl has left Mr. Tennyson's belfry, and is sailing with noiseless wings over the fields, seeking for mice to sustain the five wits with which he is accredited by the poet. And so trout fishing has its romantic side, as other apparently prosaic things are also reported to have; but the practical division of the art is perhaps acquired with more ease and satisfaction by the majority of people to whom morning, noon, and dusk bring appetite, digestion, and sleep, unembarrassed by the picturesque suggestions of persons of lymphatic temperaments, who cannot buy a trout from the fishmonger without subjecting themselves to memories of flirtation, and woods, and owls, and other irrelevant impertinences.

U

CHAPTER III.

ALTHOUGH on some rivers trout fishing com-
mences in March, those who follow the
pursuit as a fine art prefer to wait till later in
the season.   By this they lose many chances of
heavy creels.   The fish at this time are not
cunning in the detection of the lures thrown
out for their capture.

Every stream, as I have said before, has a
character of its own, has its good month and
its bad month, but fair sport may be had
occasionally during cold weather, before spring
has quite lost the chill of winter.   Nay,
even in a snow storm (before the stream
gets the colour of snow-water) it is possible to
have good fortunes in the gentle recreation.
The variety, the coquettishness, so to speak, of
rivers, renders it exceedingly difficult to lay
down laws of wide application for trout fishing.
Of course, you must acquire the first principles
of the craft; and they are not to be learned out
of a book.   The tyro, spending his days and
nights in piscatorial treatises, will go next day

and walk the stream until there cometh the ominous crack denoting that his flies have been sent into space, or until the rod is broken at the top joint while the owner is endeavouring to break off the limb of a distant hawthorn. There is nothing, indeed, for Mr. Briggs, but an apprenticeship, and private rehearsals, say, in a lawn or garden, carried on with the secrecy with which middle-aged people endeavour to acquire a new dance. Let him first practise without flies, as recruits are made to fire off powder without ball. It must be remembered, that to be a good trout angler requires absolutely more science in many respects than to be famous for the use of the salmon rod. The effects of the latter are on a larger and coarser scale. Not that the art of salmon fishing is simple, or to be acquired without much toil and taste; what we mean is that trout fishing is to salmon fishing what a delicate cabinet picture is to a bold rough landscape painting.

And firstly, the angler who condescends to use worms for trout, or any bait save the artificial fly, is a mere pot-fisher, notwithstanding Walton and other more recent authorities to the contrary. When you cannot rise the trout with flies there is great propriety in leaving them where they are. No gentleman should ever permit himself to be reconciled to worms and their abominations. They are of disagreeable origin, and unsavoury altogether. Nor when you have impaled them on a hook, is their wriggling a cheerful sight. To the use of the natural fly there are similar objections, and it is also suggestive of poaching. Sneaking behind a bush and dropping a kicking bluebottle over the nose of a feeding trout is a piece of strategy with a meanness about it. Men who cannot fill their baskets otherwise may resort to contrivances permissible in the early ages of the art, but surely they should be forbidden to those who aspire to win professorial degrees in it. And touching the question of artificial flies, we believe with a shrewd Scotchman, that, although the fish regard them as food of some sort, they never mistake them for the particular creature they are intended to imitate. An immense amount of rubbish has been written on this point. You frequently read of a typical

angler who never puts up a cast until he comes
to the brink of the stream. Arrived there, he
studies the colour of the fly then on the water,
and opening his book proceeds to construct
an animal as like it as possible. If the trout
are on the feed, and this personage knows how
to throw his line, there is no doubt he may be
successful ; but if the fish are not rising, all his
skill will serve him little. Flies look different
in the water according to the manner in which
they are played and fished. If, for instance,
you whisk a fly two or three times through the
air before dropping it in the brook in order to
dry it, and it is then kept well on the sur-
face of the stream, it will appear, for a while
at least, much as it did in the shopman's case ;
if, on the other hand, you let it sink (as is
often advisable), it wears quite another aspect.
Various rivers have their favourite flies and
colours, no doubt, but not nearly to the extent
imagined by simple tackle-makers. Any stream
may be attacked with confidence with half a
dozen sets of flies. The grand secret is really
to ascertain at what hour of the morning or
midday the trout are in the habit of feeding.

Although the seasons may help you to give a proximate guess as to the period, nothing but experience of your own or the borrowed experience of another, will put you in possession of the exact time. Fishing between it or after it is a work of supererogation. An odd trout may be hooked, but the chances are that it will be a small and foolish one, with more curiosity than discretion, and full of raw greediness untempered by age or weight. When the feeding time is ascertained, it is only an incapable who fails to have good sport. Of course the incapable can manage at any hour of the day to drive the fish before him like sheep, while he flogs the river over their heads, and sends them scuttling off as swiftly as shadows. One way he has of doing this is to come as close to the bank as he can, and fish with the stream. The effect of this ingenious manœuvre is that, as all the fish have their heads up stream, they can scarce fail to see the incapable, his rod, his flies, his uniform, and all the rest of it. It is almost impossible to cure a bad angler of the stupid custom to which I refer, and for the reason that, fishing

in this style, the current plays the casting line
for him nicely, and in a manner which he
thinks irresistible. It is scarcely necessary to
observe that the chances of taking a trout are
multiplied by approaching him from behind
and letting your flies drop naturally across
him. Except for small trout in a brook, a
beck, or a mountain streamlet, there is not
much use in performing *tremolo* movements
with the rod. Big trout do not care for such
trifling; and for them also, unless the weather
be very warm, let your flies sink well below
the surface. With regard to the spots for
trout, it is a good plan, if the river is not large,
to survey it carefully without a rod when the
water is low and clear. You are pretty sure
to note the big trout near their haunts, and
may feel assured that they will not desert them
when the stream rises. It is often quite use-
less to try tempting-looking reaches of a
stream; for some cause or other the fish never
remain near them. On the other hand, every
river has its "finds," in which you will be sel-
dom thrown out or disappointed, if you ap-
proach them at the right hour and with due

care.   The edge of a rock or stone, the trunk
of an old tree, the part below a waterfall where
the stream has turned from clear colour to a
clear bubbling brown, are favourite spots for
trout.   If there is one large trout at any of
these places, however, you will seldom get a
second until a few days pass by, when the post
of the monster is filled up by an equally satis-
factory successor.   Should the run of fish be
small in the stream, dozens may be picked out
one after another below waterfalls.

Fly-fishing in the neighbourhood of trees,
except to a genuine artist, is the parent of
cursing or of sullen discontent, which some-
times ends in the gnashing of teeth, the smash-
ing of rods, and other expressions of despair.
To be sure, big trout seek inaccessible re-
treats, but you are seldom compensated for
the trouble involved in their capture.   Not
the least pleasure in trout fishing is that it
leads you into sweet paths and walks.   This
it is which has made so many writers rave
about a pastime of which they know nothing,
but of which they feel as many infinite things
as a sucking poet does.

Lake fishing for trout, with cross-lines, is not to be commended ; it is too murderous. Besides, it is a joint-stock affair, and trout fishing is a jealous and solitary sport. Lake fishing in any style, save for the size of the fish, is stupid work, whether effected from a boat or from the bank. It does not afford nearly the variety or interest of stream angling. With reference to times and temperatures for trout fishing, I must admit that as yet the meteorological data are imperfect for the rigid definition of principles. It used to be said that trout never rose while there was thunder in the air, but the dogma is about as valuable as the supposed consequence of the same electric condition of the atmosphere upon the small ale in cellars. Then trout would not feed after a flood, when the water was too high. They also abstained from flies and grubs when the water was too low, or when the days were cold. Not one of these statements can be rationally justified, although some of them are true, but only of some rivers. A thorough master of his art ought to be able to engage by hook or by crook (bar worms and their re-

x

latives of all degrees), to make a full basket on a good stream within the twenty-four hours. If other times fail him, there is (late in the season) the evening. This is a delightful hour for angling, when the sun has gone behind the hills and the water is becoming grey, shot here and there with unexpected lights. Ply closely the shallows; as the darkness comes on the heavy trout leave the deep holes and feed in parts of the stream where there is scarce water enough to cover them. Your tackle must be strong, for it is necessary to be more or less independent of a landing net. Be careful that you fish a clear part of the river, as a tangle or a fixture at such a period almost certainly involves the loss of a casting line. These are only a few wrinkles in the craft of trout fishing; they have been picked up by the running brooks. Let not the aspirant think to learn this art by graduating in a punt on the Thames. No cockney with his bait-bag can ever become a genuine trout or salmon fisher. His appetite has been spoiled by the taking of those coarse fish who haunt the locks and skulk about the nasty little towns between London and Oxford.

By and by, perhaps, Thames trout, through Mr. Buckland's exertions, will be frequent in that river; but at present those who desire to angle for the fish must find a stream unpolluted by factories and somewhat removed from railway stations.

PRINTED BY TAYLOR AND CO.,
LITTLE QUEEN STREET, LINCOLN'S INN FIELDS.

CPSIA information can be obtained
at www.ICGtesting.com
Printed in the USA
BVHW090932270819
556819BV00014B/3079/P

9 781318 541942